Finding Your Way
in Seminary

Finding Your Way in Seminary

What to Expect, How to Thrive

David M. Mellott

WJK WESTMINSTER
JOHN KNOX PRESS
LOUISVILLE • KENTUCKY

First edition
Published by Westminster John Knox Press
Louisville, Kentucky

16 17 18 19 20 21 22 23 24 25—10 9 8 7 6 5 4 3 2 1

Unless otherwise indicated, Scripture quotations are from the New Revised Standard Version of the Bible, copyright © 1989 by the Division of Christian Education of the National Council of the Churches of Christ in the U.S.A., and are used by permission.

Scripture quotations marked CEB are from The New English Bible, © 2011 Common English Bible.

Book design by Drew Stevens
Cover design by Allison Taylor
Cover photo: The William Smith Morton Library
on the campus of Union Presbyterian Seminary, Richmond, Virginia.
Used by permission of Union Presbyterian Seminary.

Library of Congress Cataloging-in-Publication Data

Names: Mellott, David M., author.
Title: Finding your way in seminary : what to expect, how to thrive / David
   Mellott.
Description: First edition. | Louisville, KY : Westminster John Knox Press,
   2016. | Includes index. | Description based on print version record and
   CIP data provided by publisher; resource not viewed.
Identifiers: LCCN 2016022067 (print) | LCCN 2016012180 (ebook) | ISBN
   9781611647600 (ebk.) | ISBN 9780664259501 (alk. paper)
Subjects: LCSH: Theology--Study and teaching--United States. |
   Theology--Study and teaching--Canada.
Classification: LCC BV4030 (print) | LCC BV4030 .M45 2016 (ebook) | DDC
   230.071/173--dc23
LC record available at https://lccn.loc.gov/2016022067

♾ The paper used in this publication meets the minimum requirements of the American National Standard for Information Sciences—Permanence of Paper for Printed Library Materials, ANSI Z39.48-1992.

Most Westminster John Knox Press books are available at special quantity discounts when purchased in bulk by corporations, organizations, and special-interest groups. For more information, please e-mail SpecialSales@wjkbooks.com.

In honor of
my parents, Joyce and Francis;
my brother and sister, Joe and Sharon;
and the love of my life, Lance, and our canine daughter, Sophie.

Contents

Foreword

This book has been written in an interesting moment. Both the church and higher education are questioning old conventions and experimenting with new practices. While higher education has retained all its traditional expressions, it has learned how to educate by distance-education strategies, how to educate for competencies, and how providers that do not function like traditional schools can be educational providers with colleges and universities. The church shows the same mixture of old and new. Some congregations are holding on to traditional practices, while others are developing new patterns of worship, ministry, and congregational organization. Denominations are undergoing transformations in the structures by which ministry is ordered and congregational efforts are organized.

Seminaries live directly at the intersection of the church and higher education; as a result, they get a double portion of the questioning and experimenting. All these changes and the responses of theological schools make contemplating a ministerial vocation and choosing a seminary more complex.

A generation or so ago, it appeared as if things were simpler and, as a result, as if choices were easier. Candidates for ministry or priesthood were often identified earlier in life, went to the seminary of their denomination, and served in predictable expressions of ministry after graduating. It was never exactly that simple, but it was more like that pattern than anything that exists presently.

Today, people consider ministry at very different moments and career stages in life, and they consider very different forms of ministry—from pastoral ministry and congregational service, to counseling, to work in nonprofit human service agencies and social justice agencies, to church planting, to ministry in a variety of institutional contexts, to international ministry and mission service. Ministry has more options, church has more forms, and theological schools are more diverse and offer more programs than they ever have before.

The multiple-everything world of theological education and

ministry needs a map so that people can find their way among many options, and David Mellott has provided a comprehensive and helpful map—exactly the resource that is needed. *Finding Your Way in Seminary* provides a wide range of information about considering seminary, experiencing seminary education, and anticipating service in the varied contexts that are informed by theological study.

Changes and multiple options are not the only characteristics this map of theological education describes. Some striking consistencies are evident as well. People continue to pursue theological education because of some stirring of faith or divine invitation. Most enter seminary because they sense a religious call, or because they want a vocation of meaning, or because they want to contribute to social good and meeting human needs—or because they are not sure about any of these reasons but are religiously motivated to explore them. The education of religious leaders has taken many forms over the two-thousand-year history of the Christian movement. But across those millennia, that education has consistently given attention to the study of ancient texts and their origins, history, and interpretation. It has attended to the practices by which religious leadership is exercised, such as preaching and liturgy, teaching and pastoral care. And it has cultivated the capacity for theological reflection.

This capacity for theological reflection contributes to a theological vision of life and faith—a kind of wisdom that accrues from looking seriously at good and evil, hope and despair, grace and judgment. This theological vision provides an interpretive guide for the work of ministry. It is the basis for meaning that is required to be with people in the routine, day-to-day moments of life, as well as in the unspeakably painful and uniquely joyful ones.

Maps identify where cities, lakes, and mountains are in a region. They do not identify, however, which parts of the cities are the most interesting, which views of the lakes are most scenic, or which of the mountains is most majestic. These kinds of descriptions require an interpretive guide. *Finding Your Way in Seminary* provides an interpretive guide in addition to a map, and the framework for this guide is theological reflection. David Mellott helps the reader understand that decision making about theological education and the processes of theological learning are themselves best understood as acts of theological reflection. He invites people to think about theological education by using its primary process and its most desired outcome—the ability to think about life and faith in fundamentally theological ways.

This book will be read in an interesting moment in the reader's life. Persons drawn to reading this book likely are considering vocational ministry and are thinking about choosing a theological school to attend or are in seminary and trying to reframe the role and purpose of their theological education. For some people. the amount of change in churchly practices and the changing cultural status of religion discourage them from pursuing ministry or theological education. The opposite response, however, is likely the better one. Because there is so much change, congregations and parishes, church-related agencies, and a wide array of other ministry contexts need leaders who are committed to their religious vision, who are courageous in those commitments, and who see in the future, whatever its shape, the home for an ancient and long-lived religious tradition that continues to renew itself.

Daniel O. Aleshire

Acknowledgments

My theological education and reflection on it began in the kitchen of my childhood home. Because our family was part Roman Catholic and part Christian Church (Disciples of Christ), we were always comparing, debating, and scrutinizing what we were experiencing. We dissected sermons and deconstructed prayer texts. My mother, who is a lifetime member of the Christian Church (Disciples of Christ), unknowingly taught us reader-response criticism every time she interpreted for us the prayers that she heard when she went to mass with us. I'm surprised that all three of us children didn't become ministers. Thank you, Mom, Dad, Joe, and Sharon. Your love, support, and wisdom have nourished me every day of my life.

Throughout my life I have received support from many institutions and communities of faith: St. Mary's Roman Catholic Church (Shadyside, Ohio); the Diocese of Steubenville; the First Christian Church (Disciples of Christ) (Shadyside); the Pontifical College Josephinum (Columbus); the American College (Leuven, Belgium); the Catholic Community of Ironton; the Society of St. Sulpice; St. Mary's Seminary and University (Baltimore); the Graduate Division of Religion of Emory University; Lancaster Theological Seminary; and Wisdom's Table at St. Peter's UCC (Lancaster, Pennsylvania). Each of these communities has contributed to my life and how I understand seminary formation and theological education.

I'm deeply grateful to the many individuals beyond my family who have supported me and my passion for theological studies and seminary formation in my early years: Fr. Bob Borer; the Rev. Paul Johnson; Sr. Claudia Bronsing, OSF; Fr. Peter Sartori; Fr. Dennis Ricker; Sr. Agnes Crone, SCN; Dr. Cecile Gray; Dr. Fina Kroenenberg; Bishop Albert Ottenweller; Msgr. Gerald Durst; Msgr. Leonard Fick; Fr. Leo Stelton; Dr. Michael Gilligan; Fr. Rick Friedrichs; Fr. John Petro; Fr. Aurileus Boberek, OSB; Sr. Dorothy Landers, OP; Fr. Vincent Chávez; Br. Simon-Hoà Phan, OSB; Fr. Gerald McBrearity, SS; Fr. David Thayer, SS; Fr. Jerry Brown, SS; Fr. Mel Blanchette, SS;

Dr. Helen Buss Mitchell; Dr. Mark Jordan; Dr. Wendy Farley; the Rev. Dr. Bobbi Patterson; the Rev. Dr. Don Saliers; and Dr. Joyce Flueckiger.

Since 2005 I have served on the faculty of Lancaster Theological Seminary. My faculty and staff colleagues have supported me and have invited me to share my gifts in ways that I never imagined. I'm grateful to each of them and all of them for the trust that they have placed in me: Dr. Julia O'Brien, Dr. Greg Carey, Dr. Lee Barrett, Dr. Anne Thayer, Deaconess Myka Kennedy Stephens, the Rev. Dr. Stephanie Crumpton, the Rev. Dr. Elizabeth Soto, the Rev. Ruth-Aimée Belonni-Rosario, Elizabeth Bennett, and Crystal Mills. I'm also appreciative of the support that I received from colleagues who no longer serve on the Lancaster faculty or staff, most particularly the late Rev. Dr. Frank Stalfa.

The Rev. Dr. Riess Potterveld, the Rev. Dr. Anabel Proffitt, the Rev. Dr. Bruce Epperly, the Rev. Dr. Ed Aponte, the Rev. Ken Daniel, and the Rev. Dr. Carol Lytch created opportunities for me to think more deeply about theological education and my role in it. Thank you for seeing my potential and for giving me opportunities to exercise leadership.

The people who have influenced the creation of this book more than anyone else are my students, past and present. When I began my first seminary faculty position, I was thirty years old and had little teaching experience. My own ten years of seminary formation were crucial to my understanding of what happens to a person during theological studies, but my students expanded my world and deepened my thinking. Students at Lancaster Seminary continue to teach me each day. In all honesty, some of my students, the graduating class of 2016 at Lancaster Theological Seminary, are the ones who charged me with the writing of this book. They were unhappy with the available texts for their introduction to seminary and expressed their expectation that I should write a new textbook! I owe this book to their mandate and their confidence in me. I am particularly grateful to several students who reviewed early versions of some of the material in this book: Tekoa, Jack, and Edward. Their feedback was tremendously helpful.

The Rev. Lance Mullins, the Rev. Emily Schwenker, and Ms. Cheryl DeMarco read portions of the manuscript and offered their expert advice. Thank you for your careful reading and wise counsel.

Most of my best friends today are friends that I made in seminary. I can't imagine life without them. Kurt, we began our theological conversations over twenty-five years ago, and I'm grateful that they continue to this day. Your friendship continues to sustain me. Thank you.

Thank you, Michael, for your mentorship and for support for over thirty years. Many of the opportunities that I have received are thanks to you. Patricia, you have been a faithful friend and colleague for over fifteen years. Thank you for helping me to believe that I have something to offer the world of theological education.

Dan, your leadership in theological education has served as a beacon in this time of great change and innovation. I'm honored that you have contributed the foreword to this book and are willing to be associated with this project.

Robert Ratcliff and the editorial staff of Westminster John Knox Press have provided excellent support and guidance. Thank you for the time and effort that you have invested in me and this project.

Finally, this book wouldn't have been possible in any way without the love, patience, and theological gifts of my husband, Lance. In his love I have found healing, refuge, and joy. Thank you, Lance, for teaching me the ways of love, the greatest gift we can share.

Introduction

The world is bigger than our experience of it. Even if we have traveled to every continent, sailed every sea, and climbed every mountain, there is still more that we can learn about the world. If we have been good students of it, we have come to understand this truth: no matter how much we learn about our world, there is still more to discover.

The same is true for the church; it's much bigger than our experience of it. No matter how diverse our background may be, and no matter how many years we have attended a church, the fullness of the church is more profound than our experience of it. It's true that many churches hold a few things in common, but each community of faith has a history and set of relationships that shape its actions and life. If we have ever visited churches other than our own, we are quick to realize that there are hymns, prayers, practices, and preaching styles that are not like the ones in our home church.

We can be thankful that God is also bigger than our experience. Whether we have sought a relationship with God for years or we began yesterday, there is more to God than what we have read, heard, or come to believe. While some may say that they like what they know about God, I believe that all of us count on God being considerably more vast than our little ideas and thoughts.

These truths point to what I think makes theological education important in every age. It's not that we need a theological education to do ministry. We need a theological education so that we can do ministry well and do it without relying solely on our limited experiences and ideas. If we haven't studied how believers have struggled throughout the centuries with ideas of God's judgment and God's mercy, we are likely to minister solely out of our particular history. If we haven't studied how our ancestors dealt with their own failures in faith, how will we know what we might do when we are seduced by the powers and principalities of this world?

A theological education does even more than help us to have a deeper knowledge of the world, the church, and God. It helps us know ourselves more thoroughly, because we too are bigger than what we know of ourselves. Praise God for that! Immersing oneself in theology is a holistic experience. Our body, mind, spirit, race, ethnicity, gender, sexual orientation, economic situation, denominational affiliation, religious heritage, and nationality will all be included in the work. There are very few educational experiences that involve a person to this extent. Identifying our location in theological conversations is more crucial than we usually imagine. Our faith attests that God meets us where we are, not where we ought to be. If this is true, then a central task of our theological reflection is to carefully identify and understand just where we are in the journey of our lives.

Whether you decide to live on campus, commute to campus, or enroll in an online program, seminary is an experience of tremendous grace and challenge for those who are called to participate in it. This book is meant to help you consider, discern, and decide if pursuing a theological education is for you. While the book does offer perspectives informed by contemporary scholarship, it is primarily a practical guide to help you successfully navigate the discernment process, the application process, the degree program, and the job-search process.

There are many different types of programs where one can study theology. Not all of them are degree programs, and not all of them are accredited degrees. I suggest in chapters 2 and 3 what to think about as you consider your options. Some of you may not be ready to enter a graduate-degree program. There are shorter and less complex learning opportunities that you can explore. Look at a variety of seminaries and ask about the various types of programs they offer. You may find it helpful to begin with an introductory course in a lifelong learning program designed for adults.

Chapter 2 of this book concentrates on schools accredited by the Association of Theological Schools, referred to as ATS. Some programs are available that are not accredited by ATS. Some of them are very good, and new schools receive accreditation each year. Much of what I have written applies to nonaccredited schools and would be helpful when looking at those programs as well.

I limited my review of degree programs to ATS schools for two main reasons. First, accredited schools have to demonstrate on a regular basis to the public and to their institutional peers that they follow the best commonly held standards. Accreditation doesn't mean that a school is perfect, but it does mean that it holds itself accountable. The second reason that I focus on ATS member schools is that if a student is interested in pursuing further education beyond the master's level, graduating from an accredited school is important. Doctoral programs and other graduate programs prefer applicants who have succeeded in schools that follow the best practices in the field of theology and religion. Some denominations also require a theological degree from an ATS-accredited school.

The book has three basic movements. Chapters 1–3 are devoted to helping you figure out if going to seminary is the right thing for you at this moment of your life. Within the chapters you'll find discernment exercises and things to consider when making your decision. Chapters 4–7 are devoted to helping you make the most out of your seminary experience. I've arranged the material around the three main dimensions of degree programs that support ministry in theologically related fields: what you need to know; what you need to be able to do; and what kind of person you need to be. Chapter 7 focuses on the experience of those who decide to enter theological studies while pastoring a church. I think much of what is discussed in this chapter, nonetheless, applies to most students in theological degree programs today. Chapter 8 will help you with the job-search process, including suggestions for creating a portfolio of your work, a résumé, and a cover letter. The chapter also walks you through the interview process and the negotiation of your employment agreement. Don't wait until you are ready to graduate to read this chapter. Some of what you need to do to find a job after graduation begins during your first year of studies.

If you have picked up this book, it's likely that you are ready to learn more about God and what it means to have faith in God. You may or may not consider yourself a person of faith, but you want to know more about what faith is and what it means to be faithful. Some of you believe that God is calling you into ministry. Most of you have someone in your life who has confirmed your yearning to know God, to learn more about God, or to respond to God's calling. Pursuing a theological education will offer you incredible access to what people have thought, said, and debated about God. It will expose you to what followers have done in the name of God. At its core, however, seminary is an invitation to know God, the world, and yourself better. This book will help you get the most out your engagement with theological education.

I began my first theology degree at the age of twenty-two. Attending seminary enriched my relationship with God, expanded my understanding of God, and brought meaning to my life in ways that I could never have imagined. Studying theology hasn't answered all my questions, but it has helped me to respond to God's call.

I rejoice that I'm able to introduce you to the seminary world and to theological studies. May God bless you abundantly each step of the way!

1

Searching for a Meaningful Life

Annie Dillard, in her book *The Writing Life*, explores how someone begins a profession, how it enters a person's body. In her exploration she shares,

> A well-known writer got collared by a university student who asked, "Do you think I could be a writer?"
>
> "Well," the writer said, "I don't know. . . . Do you like sentences?"
>
> The writer could see the student's amazement. Sentences? Do I like sentences? I am twenty years old and do I like sentences? If he had liked sentences, of course, he could begin, like a joyful painter I knew. I asked him how he came to be a painter. He said, "I liked the smell of the paint."

I have shared this passage with many people over the years and have asked them what they would ask of the person who inquired, "Do you think I could be a pastor?" How would they fill in this question, "I don't know. . . . Do you like _____?"

"God," "conflict," "people," "the Bible," "listening," "human frailty," and "meetings" are among the answers that I have gotten. But I don't think that's how one begins. Dillard's story suggests that the initial attraction should be more basic, primal, and pleasurable. These items sound like what a pastor is *supposed* to like at the beginning.

There isn't one way to fill in this question. At the moment, I would reply to the person who asked if I thought the person could be a pastor, "I don't know. Do you like <u>metaphor</u>?"

As you are reading this, you may respond to my question like the student above inquiring about being a writer: "Do I like *metaphor*? I don't want to be an English teacher. I asked about being a minister. Do I like metaphor? I don't get it."

At its heart, ministry requires a comfort, dexterity, and fascination with using words from one context to better understand another context. That's what metaphor is. Every time we talk about God, we use metaphors. It's all we have to talk about the Power, the Being, the One that upholds everything. All we have is metaphor to describe what is indescribable.

If you like metaphor, you'll be able to begin reading the Bible and listening for the numerous metaphors used for God: song, creator, lily of the valley, rose of Sharon, ancient of days, lord, sun, bridegroom, father of lights, shade, shepherd of Israel, spring of living water, and so forth.

If you like metaphor, you can begin listening for the many words and expressions that people use when talking about Christianity: heavenly, yoke, deliverance, born again, mother of God, land of milk and honey, resurrected, the lamb of God, dying with Christ, and so on.

If you like metaphor, you can start to appreciate the diversity of religious experience and expression that exists within a religious community and among the various religious communities around the world. You'll be able to hear the variations of God language: mother, bagworm, ultimate reality, daddy God, cosmic controller, clockmaker, architect of the universe, and many others.

If you like metaphor, you'll be able to listen for the subtleties that lie within the metaphors used in the questions that haunt us. How do you measure a year in one's life? That's the question that the Broadway show *Rent* explores in its popular song "Seasons of Love." The show tune offers a number of metaphors in response: daylights, sunsets, cups of coffee, inches, miles, the bridges that we burned, the way that we died, seasons of love.

The song and its extravagant use of metaphor taps into something poignant about being human. We all ask questions about our experiences, both individual and communal experiences. We may be asking, "Who am I becoming?" "What season am I in right now?" "How do I get out of this wilderness?" "Why is life such a feast for some and so bankrupt for others?" "Why does God smile on some but not on others?" "Why is love such a battlefield?"

Underneath all these metaphors is our desire to understand our human experience more deeply. Trying various metaphors and testing their ability to help us understand our lives and the world around us is fundamental to being human. We want to know if our lives have any meaning. We want our lives to matter, to make a difference—to our families, our friends, God, the world, ourselves. We are also compelled to make sense of the issues and challenges that face us communally as well as individually. Stories of disease, war, racism, environmental catastrophe, greed, sexism, classism, and heterosexism surround us and compel us to wonder what we can do to address the issues that plague our world. In addition to our role in finding solutions, we wonder about God's role.

The metaphors that we use as we go about making meaning for our lives and exploring these human problems depend on a number of factors: age, national context, family background, sexual identity, gender, economic status, place of residence, race, ethnicity, individual history, education, religious tradition. Furthermore, *how* we bring all these factors together in our lives is one way in which we create meaning for our life.

Major societal and personal experiences emerge, destabilizing our language and meaning making. Sometimes these interruptions force us to rethink where we are going. New ideas, new experiences, and new relationships all have the power to call into question the choices we have made. The metaphors under which we were living can fall apart. A story that we had been telling to ourselves and to others about who we are and what is important to us can fail to satisfy. We wonder who we are and how we got here.

Beneath and behind the work of ministers is an attraction to the language, questions, and struggles of the human heart and to understanding how God and we have navigated those things over time. This is theological work. At its heart, the work of Christian theology is an active exploration of what it means to be human. That means that it involves practice, study, reflection, and transformation.

Seminary is the best place to explore these interests. It's not the only place where that should be happening. Ideally it occurs in every community, family, congregation, and denomination. But in seminaries and other schools of theology it more often happens at the depth that changes lives and quickens a person's vocational path.

The truth is that most people don't arrive at seminary with a clear sense of what they want to do with their degree. Many are interested in thinking about some form of ministry, congregational ministry in particular. But most seminarians are far less settled on the question of what they imagine to be their future vocation. In fact, this vagueness has increased over the years. People have more vocational choices than our ancestors did just a few decades ago.

Even when attending seminary was associated solely with the pursuit of becoming an ordained clergy person, people were more fluid in their vocational aspirations than many think. One of the reasons for this was that the seminary process demanded that students examine every aspect of their lives, including their motivations, dreams, values, and weaknesses. No one emerges from that experience unchanged. Some ended up pursuing other professions yet still carrying the skills and dispositions that they cultivated in seminary.

To begin your theological studies, then, you don't need to be able to say that you want to be a pastor or an ordained minister. Theological schools do more than prepare people for a variety of ministries in the world. They help you to explore what it means to be human. They help you become yourself. If you are drawn to the beauty of metaphors and the stirrings of the human heart, God may be inviting you to take the next step in your discipleship by entering into deeper theological reflection.

THEOLOGICAL EDUCATION
AND THEOLOGICAL REFLECTION

There are many formal components of theological education, which we'll review in chapter 2. At its core I would propose that theological education is dominated by the exposure of students to the history of Christian thought and practice, with the aim of helping students make their own response to God and walk their own path of faith. No one can live the life of faith for us. We must do it ourselves. I don't mean that we do it on our own. To the contrary, we do it in the community of believers who are with us now and who have gone before us. We need the wisdom of others to guide us, but they can't make the choices for us. Only we can take responsibility for our lives.

To put it another way, theological education is an initiation into the ongoing conversation with God, others, and ourselves. The process is complex, involving many languages, cultures, and forms of communication. Participation in the conversation and reflection on that participation are required. Theological education, then, is built on the practice of theological reflection.

Patricia O'Connell Killen and John de Beer, authors of *The Art of Theological Reflection*, define theological reflection as

> the discipline of exploring individual and corporate experience in conversation with the wisdom of a religious heritage. The conversation is a genuine dialogue that seeks to hear from our own beliefs, actions, and perspectives, as well as those of the tradition. It respects the integrity of both. Theological reflection therefore may confirm, challenge, clarify, and expand how we understand our own experience and how we understand the religious tradition. The outcome is new truth and meaning for living.[1]

This is all to say that each of us has participated in what Christianity calls *theological reflection*, even if we haven't called it that. Whenever we have sought to understand our experience, to explore the language that we use to describe that experience, or to address the condition of our lives in the light of our own personal history and our religious traditions, we have engaged in theological reflection.

There are a number of models for theological reflection, but all of them involve a conversation between individual and corporate experiences and the resources of our religious traditions.[2] The Bible, the lives of the saints, church history, poetry, stories, church teachings, and hymns are among those resources.

Most of us, however, have more experiences and questions than we have exposure to our religious heritage or to the skills needed to understand those resources. Maybe we have gone to church, Sunday school, or catechism classes. We may have gone to church camp or taken introductory courses in religion in college. At some point we realize that our familiarity with our religious tradition is not sufficient for engaging our questions. The ideas, language, stories, and perspectives we received from our classes, churches, parents, and mentors are helpful, but they leave us wanting more. We know that we aren't the first people to ask these questions or to struggle with these problems. It would be helpful to know how our ancestors and contemporaries in our religious heritage wrestled with these questions, to know what language they used, and to know the impact of the decisions that they made.

This is why theological education is so important, necessary, and exciting. We are able to bring our own experience, language, and choices to a much larger conversation that has been happening for millennia. We find colleagues, conspirators, and collaborators—people with whom we can study, breathe, and act together. Theological education gives us the tools to pay attention to the metaphors we use for God, the world, and ourselves. On understanding our own religious experience and the language that we use, we can explore the experiences and languages of others, which will lead us into a place where we are empowered to make choices about our lives and about the language we will use to describe our lives. Through the rigorous examination of our own religious lexicon, we begin to comprehend the impact of our language for God. We get a glimpse of how our language doesn't simply reflect how we think and act; it also *shapes* how we think and act. This is to say, there are ethical consequences to our language. Some metaphors bear good fruit. Others, most certainly not. We are responsible for how we talk, most especially when we attempt to speak about those things that ultimately can't be limited or defined through our speech. This includes God.

THE MOVEMENTS OF THEOLOGICAL REFLECTION

At its heart, theological reflection is not about problem solving, because life isn't a problem to be solved. That's not to say that problems aren't examined using theological reflection but the ultimate intention is to listen carefully for God as we go about making choices in our life. Theological reflection, then, is a matter of exploring, developing, and strengthening our relationship with God, self, and others. We may not be able to resolve a problem, but we can make a choice to accept God's invitation to us, regardless of where it may seem to take us.

The process is typically ignited by an experience, leads us into deeper insight about our lives, and inspires us to another way of being in the world.[3] The experience can be as simple as having a deep insight at the intersection of two busy streets or as complex as realizing that something gives us more joy than we ever thought possible. Regardless of the experience and its complexity, there are inner and outer dimensions to the event. What often draws our attention to those inner and outer dimensions is the feeling that is generated by the experience. Those feelings include how we bodily respond to what is happening and how we are reflecting on those physical sensations.

For example, a friend once shared with me about a time in her life when she was standing in the middle of an aisle in the grocery store.

For some reason, she became aware that she was not in her typical race through the store. For the first time in a long time, she was not in a hurry. As she stood there, she could feel her entire body relaxing. She felt happy to be able to enjoy the experience and took her time, walking slowly through the store. As feelings of happiness continued, she also felt grateful to be able to take such pleasure from the simple task of grocery shopping.

The feelings that are generated by our experiences will often give way to an image or metaphor about how we are interpreting what is happening to us. In the example above, her operating metaphor was challenged: my friend wasn't running a race, as she usually did while grocery shopping. As she reflected on her experience that day of *not* being in a race, she began to consider the other things in life that she had failed to experience, appreciate, and enjoy because she was too much in a hurry to get the task completed. The insight she reached that afternoon was that if she were willing to slow down, she might be able to enjoy more fully the life God had given her. And that joy could lead her to a deeper sense of gratitude, even for the simple things in her life.

In my own life, I have experienced numerous invitations to engage in theological reflection about my day-to-day life. A more complex invitation came to my door at the parsonage. One Sunday evening a woman who described herself as "having had too much to drink" came to the parsonage because she needed someone to drive her home, across the state line. She wanted me to find a way to get her home. As I volunteered to call her a taxi, she added that she was hungry and would also like something to eat. I agreed to find something for her to eat. When I produced an apple she refused it, indicating that she didn't have enough teeth to eat it. When I presented a banana she took it but deposited it in her coat to eat later. Since she was still in need of something to eat, I offered her a peanut butter and jelly sandwich, which she agreed would be fine, but only if the peanut butter was creamy. Her lack of teeth prevented her from eating crunchy peanut butter. Eventually, I got her fed and sent her home in the taxi. As she left, she promised that later in the week she would bring me the money for the taxi fare.

When I got back inside the parsonage, I complained to a visiting friend about how rude this woman was with me. "I went out of my way to help her, and she never even thanked me," I whined to my friend. I had no expectation that she would pay me back for the taxi, but I was annoyed that she didn't express any gratitude to me.

For the next several days I was irritated and agitated by the experience. When I prayed about it, I started to feel guilty about what I was feeling. I thought I had done a righteous deed, but I didn't feel like it.

It took me years before I realized what had happened that Sunday evening. I thought I was doing a good deed for that woman who sought my help that Sunday night. However, when I was able to be honest with myself, I realized that I didn't help her because she needed my assistance or because Jesus has commanded us to care for those who are vulnerable. I helped her in order to feel good about myself, and her lack of gratitude prevented me from thinking of myself as the "good Samaritan." Following that experience, I began to hesitate about assisting those who requested help.

What helped me to explore my experience that night and to reinterpret what happened was a passage by Thomas Merton that I read in a theology course: "But if you want to identify me, ask me not where I live, or what I like to eat, or how I comb my hair, but ask me what I think I am living for, *in detail*, and ask me what I think is keeping me from living fully for the thing that I want to live for. Between these two answers you can determine the identity of any person. The better answer he has, the more of a person he is."[4]

Merton's comments helped me to understand that even though helping this woman was appropriate, the way that I interpreted what happened was also important. In this case, my intention wasn't what I thought it had been. I thought I was trying to help her, but I wasn't. I was trying to shore up my own ego and my fragile discipleship.

Beyond getting a better understanding of my ulterior motives in that transaction that night, I realized a couple of other important matters. The first is that my response to the woman's behavior said much more about my sense of privilege and entitlement than it said about her gratitude. I didn't know anything about this woman's life, but I did expect her to be grateful for my generosity. I was sharing from my abundance, but I didn't spend any time considering that there could be a connection between my place of privilege and her place of disadvantage.

The second thing that I realized, thanks to Merton, was that I wasn't alone in my struggle to live a more authentic Christian life. Through Merton's writing, I was able to see my experience within the larger dynamic of growing in faith. My own growing self-awareness was part of the process of God inviting me to take another step in my life of discipleship. Challenged by my own mixture of motivations for ministry and inspired by the testimony of another follower of Christ, I was able to pursue my own life-changing process of exploring what I was doing with my life and why.

What are the experiences of your life that are calling you to a deeper awareness of yourself, God, and others? What are the feelings and metaphors that are emerging from your experiences? Do you have an adequate amount of knowledge about Christianity and the skills to use those resources in the service of reflecting theologically on those experiences? What invitation is God making to you? How is that invitation leading you into life-changing actions, however small or large? If you are drawn to the practice of theological reflection, God may be inviting you to take the next step in your discipleship by pursuing theological education.

DISCERNMENT AND MAKING CHOICES

Among the many elements of a mature spiritual life, few are more important than the practices of discernment and making choices. In the case of thinking about enrolling in a seminary or pursuing the vocation of authorized ministry, these practices are critical. One of the biggest challenges is that the two—discernment and making choices—are often conflated, which usually results in ignoring the practice of discernment altogether. We need to separate the practices from each other so that the power entailed in each can be honored and appreciated. Applying to and enrolling in a theology program is more than making the choice to do so. At least it should be. Before making the decision, it's important to pay attention to the various factors involved in committing to such a program.[5]

The verb *discern* comes from the Latin word *discernere*, which means "to separate" or "to distinguish." When we discern, we are actually sorting out ideas, issues, and possibilities. This process is crucial, because it helps to make sure that we are looking at all the various elements that are part of making a choice. If we don't separate out the issues, we can overlook critical information that is necessary for wise and sound choices. For example, applying to a school of theology has financial implications for the student and the family of the student. This reality can't be ignored, even if the person feels strongly about being called by God to pursue a theology degree and to serve as a pastor in a congregation. The undiscerning person could overlook the financial realities of this choice and end up jeopardizing the well-being of her or his family.

Discernment entails a gathering of all the essential pieces of information and reflecting on them. The larger the decision, the larger the discernment process will need to be. In addition, a person will need to pay close attention to each element and to assess its impact on the decision. For example, the person who is attracted to attending seminary but did not develop strong-enough learning skills to succeed in college may need some additional course work before enrolling in a graduate program. The additional course work will entail additional expense and time. This additional work doesn't mean that going to seminary is impossible; it simply means that the path will be affected.

The practice of making a choice can also be undermined when we meld it with discernment. When we make a choice, we are declaring to ourselves and to others that we are accountable for what we are doing. We may rely on information and ideas from others, but ultimately only we can make the decision. If we don't distinguish between discernment and making choices, it can be too easy for us to deny our accountability and responsibility when the path becomes challenging. If we aren't clear about the choices that we are making and why we are making them, we don't have the benefit of that clarity when we are struggling with the implications of that choice. Owning our choices brings clarity and clarity generates the energy we need to follow through with our choices. Like any big decision, engaging in a program of theological studies brings challenges to every part of our life. If we aren't clear about why we made the choice we made, we won't be able to rely on the energy that comes with having made a choice.

In this chapter we have begun the process of discernment, of attending to the questions, ideas, and experiences that pull on us for greater reflection. We've also looked at the possibility of not having enough knowledge about our Christian heritage to reflect in the way and at the depth that we would like. If you are interested in questions about what it means to be human, which includes being in relationship to God, that's important information for your discernment process.

If you are interested, there's more to consider. What kind of theological programs are available? What are the application requirements? What resources will I need? What options do I have for financing my studies? How many years will the program take? How much time each week will I need to devote to my studies? What kind of academic background is required, and am I prepared academically for graduate studies?

Who is involved in the decision-making process? How will doing the degree affect my family and household? To what extent have I invited God into my discernment process and paid attention to what God is saying to me? This isn't everything, but it's a good start.

The practice of discernment is more than creating a checklist or a list of pros and cons. It involves gathering all the pertinent information and holding it together before us. As we do, we consider who we are, what's important to us, how we want to invest our life, what the realities of the world are, and how our relationship is with God.

If you are a professional minister who has not graduated from seminary and who is reading this book, then you must already have a sense that you need to expand your theological education. You have realized on some level that God and the church are much bigger than your experience of them. You already know that if you want to enrich your relationship with God and to discern more clearly God's invitations to you and the world, attending a seminary or school of theology will provide those opportunities. The next step in your discernment process is exploring schools and degree programs.

If you are a person who is compelled to reflect theologically on your life experiences, whether you are a member of a church or not, you may want to look at what introductory courses in theology are available in your area. You can contact your pastor or the pastor of a local church and inquire about what classes they offer. You can also find out if there is a theological school in your area. Most schools have programs that allow accepted students to take a limited number of courses without applying for a degree program. Most theological schools also offer nondegree courses that are open to anyone. Check their website for continuing education or lifelong-learning programs. In both cases, these courses will help you expand your knowledge of the Christian heritage and will allow you to experience what theological education feels like. If you find yourself longing for more engagement and coursework, you can inquire about applying your completed coursework toward a degree program. I'll talk more about this in the following chapters.

Some of you have been fully engaged in theological reflection and have already taken introductory courses in theology and already know that doing theological reflection is a passion for you. You may also find it engaging to help others reflect theologically. Most likely you are eager to pursue a theological degree. What you may not know at this point is what you would *do* with a theological degree. If you entered a theological degree program without this knowledge, you wouldn't be alone. Seminary is often a place where a person realizes her or his calling. Before you jump into a program or too quickly dismiss the idea of applying to seminary, read through the remainder of this section of the book. You may be surprised by how many options there are for getting a theological degree.

Others of you have been fully engaged in theological reflection, taken some introductory courses in theology, and know that you are interested in some form of authorized Christian ministry. The next step in your discernment process is to explore the various schools and degree programs that are available.

In the next chapter we'll review the various degree programs offered, requirements affecting applications, and various teaching formats now being used in theological education. All this information will contribute to your discernment process and support your decision.

Wherever you are in your life of faith, various forms of theological education and the graces of theological reflection are available to you. All you need to do is pay attention to your life experiences and the ways that you respond to them. From there, you can engage the incredible wisdom of others on the way. The best news of all is that God can find us, wherever we are, and lead us into a wider and deeper way of living.

2

Envisioning Your Educational and Vocational Path

What kinds of theological degrees are there? Are there any degree programs in theology offered online? Are there different types of schools that offer theology degrees? These are the questions that we'll explore in this chapter, which will prepare you for the process of selecting the school and program that is best for you.

If you haven't ever looked at the degrees offered by theological schools, you may be surprised about how many different kinds of degrees are available, how many different formats are used, and how many different schools there are around the country. Currently more than 270 schools are members of the Association of Theological Schools (ATS), which accredits graduate theological schools in the United States and Canada. There are three general categories of master's-level programs, with numerous variations and distinctions within each category:

— Programs oriented toward ministerial leadership
— Programs oriented toward general theological education
— Advanced programs oriented toward theological research and teaching

Thanks to technological developments, changes in higher education, and changes by accrediting bodies, there is a larger variety of teaching formats used in these degree programs. The number of satellite classrooms and online classrooms has increased in recent years. It's important to know that some schools utilize only face-to-face courses. Others offer programs only online. Still others use a combination of online and face-to-face learning. In this chapter, we'll focus on exploring the different kinds of degrees and their components. We'll also take a closer look at the various teaching formats and how they may influence your choice of schools and programs.

MASTER'S-LEVEL DEGREE PROGRAMS IN THEOLOGY

The review of degree programs would be easier if we could say that there is a direct correspondence between a specific degree and a specific vocation. If this were true, we could create a chart where you could look up which vocation you wanted to pursue and then look for the corresponding degree. The truth is that programs oriented toward ministerial leadership, called professional degrees, are often also used as a pathway to academic vocations such as theological research and teaching. It's also true that programs oriented toward theological education, often considered academic degrees, are used in support of authorized ministerial leadership.

To complicate things further, denominations across the country have been changing their requirements for ordained or authorized ministry. Some denominations that have historically not required a theology degree for ordination are now requiring a master's degree, typically a master of divinity (MDiv) degree. Other denominations that have historically required a master of divinity degree are allowing candidates for ordination to use a shorter master's program or to enroll in a nondegree training program offered by the denomination. Despite these variations, there remains a general pattern of engaging theological degrees as the way to pursue a vocation in ministerial leadership, academic teaching, or some combination of the two.

Programs Oriented toward Ministerial Leadership

In 2006 the Carnegie Foundation for the Advancement of Teaching published *Educating Clergy: Teaching Practices and Pastoral Imagination*, the first book in a series of studies on how particular professionals are prepared for their vocations. The series includes the education of clergy, physicians, lawyers, engineers, and nurses. By looking at all these different professional paths, the researchers noted that the preparation or cultivation process focused on a combination of three apprenticeships, each focused on a specific dimension of the vocation:

> The cognitive apprenticeship, which addresses *what one needs to know* for the particular vocation;
>
> The practical apprenticeship, which addresses *what one needs to be able to do* for a particular vocation;
>
> The identity formation apprenticeship, which addresses *what kind of person* one needs to be for the particular vocation.[1]

Most seminaries or schools of theology won't use the language of the three apprenticeships, but they certainly would understand these as the main dimensions of any MDiv degree program. The three apprenticeships show up across a curriculum. Each school crafts a curriculum with its own balance and emphasis on the apprenticeships. Some apprenticeships may receive more attention in one program than they do in others. Knowing some of the details of each apprenticeship will help you know what to expect in an MDiv program and what questions to ask when looking at different schools.

Degree programs oriented toward ministerial leadership are the theological degree programs that prepare people either for general pastoral ministry or for a specialized form of pastoral ministry. Pastoring a congregation, serving as a chaplain, or working in some types of denominational offices are examples of general pastoral ministry. Christian education, music, pastoral counseling, and youth and young-adult ministries are examples of specialized pastoral ministries.

The Master of Divinity

The MDiv degree is the standard professional degree for general authorized ministerial leadership. The MDiv is the most sought-after theological degree at the master's level in ATS accredited schools. In 2013, some 54 percent of the master's-level students were in MDiv degree programs.[2] Because it is the most prominent theological degree program, the general components of this degree will provide the clearest picture of what you need to consider when analyzing your options.

The Cognitive Apprenticeship

There is a lot of information that a minister is supposed to know. In fact, there is more to know about Christianity, its history, and its practices than any one person can know. Consequently, knowing how and where to find information and how to interpret it is particularly important. Ministers are expected to have a general knowledge of the Bible, events and people in Christian history, the various strands of Christianity, Christian worship, preaching, teaching, Christian ethics, pastoral care, spiritual practices, religions of the world, community organizing, theological doctrines, institutional organization, and church administration. Within each of these areas there are multiple interpretations, approaches, and debates occurring. Students are expected to learn about these various dimensions of theology and to practice integrating them into an approach to life, faith, and ministry.

It's not surprising that the majority of time in the MDiv program is spent on this apprenticeship. Even when kept to a minimum, the body of knowledge needed to be a minister is extensive. This apprenticeship is practiced primarily in academic coursework. The number of semester course credits that is required for the MDiv degree ranges from seventy-two to just fewer than a hundred. That's a significant range, which has recently emerged in the move by some seminaries to make the MDiv more affordable for students and seminaries.

In addition to attaining the general knowledge outlined above, students who are investigating or pursuing authorized ministry within a particular denomination will likely have additional requirements. Biblical exegesis; Latin; Greek; Hebrew; human sexuality; the history of the gay, lesbian, bisexual, and transgender community; and denominational polity are a few examples of the additional coursework that students from a particular denomination may be required to take.

The Practical Apprenticeship

The word "practical" in this context is referring to the regular actions that a minister is expected to perform. Preaching, praying, teaching, and providing pastoral care are some examples from the practice of ministry. The MDiv degree, as noted above, is a professional degree intended to prepare people to *perform* pastoral ministry. The degree isn't intended to prepare people to be academics or to teach at a university. There are other master's degrees that are crafted to prepare people for those vocations. The MDiv, then, has a distinct focus on the *practice* of ministry. A healthy school will not interpret time in the curriculum focused on the practices of ministry as secondary to or in competition with the body of information explored in the cognitive apprenticeship. These apprenticeships should complement each other. For example, the effective preacher should know how the practice has evolved in particular times and places. He or she should know what risks have been taken by preachers and to what end. They also need to be comfortable in their body and to know how to modulate their voice. These things are learned by *studying* the work of others and by *practicing*. Relying solely on one or the other is not sufficient.

Supervised Ministry/Field Education. As part of the practical apprenticeship, the MDiv degree typically involves time spent performing ministry in a supervised context. This aspect of the program is intended to instill in the minister the pattern of practice, reflection, and adjustment to one's ministry context. In some schools this is called supervised ministry. In other schools it's called field education.[3] The amount of time spent in a supervised-ministry setting varies across ATS schools. Most schools will require at least one academic year of supervised ministry with the student working around ten hours each week at the ministry-placement site. Many schools will require two academic years of supervised ministry. Very few would require more than two years. Seminary graduates often name their supervised-ministry experiences as the most critical part of their seminary education.

Examples of supervised-ministry placements include a congregation, denominational office, hospital, hospice, college classroom, nursing home, soup kitchen, campus ministry, prison, and the YWCA. Most seminaries are open to students proposing new ministry sites and will have a process by which the student can submit the request. Successful supervised-ministry placements require a talented supervisor and an open community, both committed to the education of the seminarian. Consequently, seminaries will have a series of expectations and requirements for any potential field-education site. For example, because newly hired ministry leaders and interim pastors often need to concentrate their energy on the urgent needs of their new settings, they are usually not eligible to be field education supervisors.

Each field placement will require the student to create a learning covenant with the supervisor and to engage in regular feedback and assessment. Most programs require midyear feedback forms and several types of year-end evaluations. Reflecting on one's experience and paying attention to what one is learning in field education is central to this apprenticeship. Students will be expected to practice integrating what they are learning in the field and what they are learning in the classroom.

Supervised-ministry departments will have a set of guidelines regarding field placements, supervisors, learning covenants, and evaluations. While the guidelines will vary from one program to another, the ultimate goal of providing students with a context where the practice of ministry includes deep theological reflection and learning from one's experience will be the same. Only placements where ministry is examined carefully and where students are challenged to think and act critically will be supported and authorized.

Students who are already pastoring a church while they are doing their MDiv degree are also expected to do supervised ministry. However, most programs work closely with these pastors so that this part of the program adds value to their ministry. The assumption isn't that the student pastor is performing unsatisfactorily. The assumption is that even a working pastor needs to take time to reflect theologically about what she or he is doing with someone who has more experience and with those who are impacted by their ministry.

Denominations often have expectations or requirements regarding supervised-ministry placements. For example, students who are being officially sponsored in seminary by their denomination will likely be expected to do at least one year in a congregation of the same denomination. Presbyterians are expected to do supervised ministry in a Presbyterian congregation, African Methodist Episcopal students in an AME congregation, United Methodists in a United Methodist congregation, and so on.

In sum, field education is organized and calibrated to invite the seminarian to be a reflective practitioner and to give the seminarian experience in the important pattern of practice, reflection, and adjustment.

Clinical Pastoral Education. Clinical pastoral education, better known as CPE, is an intensified form of supervised ministry. CPE programs exist in hospitals, hospices, nursing homes, prisons, and other places where pastoral care is offered. New sites for CPE programs are being explored each year. Each of these programs includes a common set of practices: didactic sessions, time working with patients or clients, theological reflection, and peer-group work.

There are a variety of programs and formats for the first unit of CPE, which is what is typically required by a seminary or denomination.

Some programs are full-time summer programs. Other programs last one or two semesters. Students intending to pursue board-certified chaplaincy will need at least four units of CPE. If you are interested in board-certified chaplaincy, you should visit the website for the Association for Clinical Pastoral Education, Inc., at www.acpe.edu for information about all the requirements.

Some MDiv programs require one unit of CPE. Other programs do not require it but will accept one unit of CPE to count toward the supervised-ministry requirements.

Practice of Ministry Courses. The practical apprenticeship also appears in the courses dedicated to the practice of ministry, specifically, preaching, worship, pastoral care, educational ministries, and church administration. These courses will likely contain a mixture of theory and practice. In addition to studying the history and the current state of these practices, students will be expected to perform practices for the review of peers and professors. Students will be expected to teach, preach, lead worship, create budgets, and offer care in simulated events. Some versions of ordained leadership include singing. In those cases, courses in music and chanting may be required and demonstration of competency in singing will be expected.

In some cases, students will need to address requisite skills before engaging some of these major practices of ministry. For example, students who are not comfortable speaking in front of others or who do not know the difference between *reading* a biblical text and *proclaiming* a biblical text will need to do some work before engaging the practice of preaching. If this is the case, students should investigate other courses in the curriculum, for example, liturgical speech or workshops that would prepare them for the major practice of ministry courses.

The Identity-Formation Apprenticeship

The identity-formation apprenticeship, according to the Carnegie study, was previously a stronger component in the education and formation of many professionals. Unfortunately, this apprenticeship no longer receives significant attention in the preparation of nurses, physicians, lawyers, and engineers. For those preparing to be priests, ministers, or rabbis, however, it remains a significant part of the educational process. In fact, the authors of *Educating Clergy* noted that the identity formation that takes place in seminaries and rabbinic schools could serve as an example for the educational programs of other professions.

This apprenticeship requires students to integrate knowledge and skills they have learned with a way of being that allows them to utilize that information for a desirable impact. The assumption is that education is more than gathering information. It's also about allowing oneself to be formed or shaped by that knowledge and being attentive to the power of that knowledge. Christianity has powerful things to say, not only about what it means to be a human being, but also about *how* to be a human being in the world. In consequence, a minister of the gospel teaches by how he or she lives in the world just as much as by what he or she says about it.

Many seminaries will identify this part of the educational process as the *formation program* of the MDiv degree. Sometimes it is called spiritual formation, sometimes ministerial formation. Some programs, particularly Roman Catholic, will address matters of "human, spiritual, and pastoral formation." Some theological schools do not have a formation program but see this as an aspect of supervised ministry. The identity-formation element of the MDiv degree is clearly the most varied across ATS schools, so it is worth paying close attention to how a theological school understands formation and carries it out.

When I was in seminary, a group of us gathered every week to play volleyball at the local gym. Week after week we had the opportunity to practice teamwork and to assess how well we did. Every week we had to face the challenge of choosing between our desires to score a point and setting up a teammate to score the point. The volleyball court was a key arena for us to work out issues of self-doubt, cooperation, trust, and faith. For me it was just as important to my education as my courses in spirituality.

Here are some elements that may be associated with the formation program of the MDiv degree.

Supervised Ministry. Just as working in the field provides an opportunity to practice particular skills and to put theological knowledge to use, it's also an opportunity to receive feedback on how our behavior impacts our ministry and interactions with others. It provides the chance to observe up close the ministry of supervisors and how they inhabit the vocation of minister. In supervised ministry, the amount of work expected is intentionally limited to allow for time to reflect theologically on each activity and responsibility. The expectation is to build up a pattern of action and reflection that will hold fast when ministerial responsibilities get heavier. The goal is to cultivate a reflective practitioner.

Course Work. Courses on the practice of prayer, discernment, spiritual formation, pastoral care, engaging conflict, and leadership all have the potential to contribute to the formation of a future minister. For example, in courses on pastoral care, students can learn about the idea of being a nonanxious presence within the context of pastoral care, and they can practice it through role-plays and interacting with seminarian colleagues.

Formation Courses. Some seminaries have courses that specifically focus on ministerial or spiritual formation. In these courses students engage in practices of prayer, nonjudgmental listening, communal discernment, giving and receiving feedback, and spiritual disciplines. These courses will also focus on listening for invitations and graces from God that arrive through these practices.

Cocurricular Activities. Numerous other activities, including mundane matters, can be part of one's theological education. These activities aren't limited to students who live in residence at the seminary. Committee work, using common laundry facilities, fundraising events, cleaning common spaces, communal work days, retreats, and sporting activities offer opportunities to learn about how we interact with others. We have these experiences within other contexts, but within the context of a formation program we do them with other people who share a commitment to listening for God and to growing in discipleship. Our peers in the program will see aspects of us that others may not see. We need them to share with us thoughtful comments about how we come across with others. They also need us to do the same for them.

Cross-Cultural Experience. Since the mid-1960s some seminaries have required an extended visit of two weeks or more to another country. Over the years more seminaries have obliged students to have this experience, because it is a powerful way for students to expand their sense of self and to identify with the concerns of the wider world. Some schools offer such experiences as electives. Typically these trips are not mission trips or service trips. They aren't vacations either. They are experiences designed to expose students to the metaphors, needs, desires, burdens, and aspirations of a people and culture not their own. Furthermore, these trips are often micro–spiritual practices, requiring

the participants to detach from their normal creature comforts, engage
the graces and constraints of living in close proximity to their peers,
and learn about how they handle conflict, disagreement, and being
"other" in a foreign land.

Worship and Prayer. All schools have some schedule of communal
worship and prayer. The quantity and types of services will be influenced
by denominational commitments of the school and often by the
composition of the student body. Students will be invited to participate
in worship planning for these services, which provides another excellent
opportunity to explore the challenges of working as a team, listening to
the insights of others, paying attention to community dynamics, and
taking on responsibilities for communal life. This type of experience
isn't limited to seminaries, but engaging in the process within this
context is different from doing it on the congregational level. Within
a formation program, participating in the planning and practice of
worship takes on additional significance. Seminarians practice taking
on the responsibility for planning and leading communal prayer and
attending to the impact of those worship experiences. As with the other
aspects of the program, seminarians do this within the context of a
common calling of excellence in spiritual leadership.

Comprehensive Midprogram Vocation Review. All seminaries have
a process for assessing students and sharing feedback with them. Some
seminaries do a minor review of all students every year. Most seminaries
do a major review midway through the MDiv degree program. The
timing and composition of this review look different across theological
schools. Ideally the midprogram review will include feedback from
peers, field supervisors, denominational leaders, and faculty members.
It should also include substantive self-assessment and reflection from
the seminarian. Students are typically expected to gather a portfolio
of artifacts: supervised ministry evaluations, self-assessments, degree
audit, transcript, theological essay or responses to theological questions,
and ministerial artifacts (sermons, lesson plans for an educational
event, personality test results, etc.). The goals for this review session
include, but are not limited to, offering the student support, assessing
the progress of the student in the program, determining readiness for
one's intended vocation, gauging the extent to which the student is
fulfilling the requirements for authorized ministry (if applicable), and
establishing what areas need additional attention by the student and
others. In these review sessions, transcripts are important, but the kind
of person, minister, leader, and Christian the student is becoming

is the focus. In sum, the midprogram review is an act of communal discernment meant to serve the student, the church, and the world. The results of the mid-program assessment are typically shared with the student's denomination if the student is in-care or officially sponsored by the denomination. In most cases, the denominational committees responsible for approving candidates for ordination take seriously the results of these processes because it gives them substantive clarity about the progress of the seminarian and his or her potential for ministry.

ATS requires a minimum of three full-time years of study or its equivalent for the MDiv. The more credits the school requires for the degree, the more credits students will need to take to complete the degree in three years. At least one year of the degree or its equivalent must be done through residential coursework at ATS schools. The other two years could be offered through distance-education coursework. However, schools are not required to offer any coursework online or through any other distance education. They are required to abide by the minimum standard and to demonstrate that the learning outcomes of the degree are being achieved.

ATS-accredited schools are permitted to accept up to 15 percent of their MDiv students without a baccalaureate degree or its equivalent. This doesn't mean that all schools accept some students without the baccalaureate. Some schools will not accept any students without the baccalaureate, and others will make exceptions only for those who have achieved the equivalency of the degree. Applicants who don't have the baccalaureate degree may be delayed in the application process while waiting for an opening to occur in the program.

Master's Degrees Oriented toward Specialized Ministry

ATS accredits numerous other master's degrees designed to prepare participants for specialized ministry. These degrees are typically called master of arts in (specialized ministry) or master of (specialized ministry). A complete listing of degrees in this category can be found on the ATS website: www.ats.edu. If you are interested in a specialized ministry, it is essential to review this listing. Global Service, Christian Formation, Aging and Spirituality, Black Church Studies, Mental Health Counseling, Counseling, Evangelism and Missions, Missional Church Studies, Christian Formation and Soul Care, Sacred Music, Urban Ministry, Family Studies, Spiritual Direction, Educational

Leadership, Youth Ministry, and Pastoral Studies are some of the specialized degrees that are being offered by accredited schools.

These master's programs require two years of study or its equivalent. Depending on the school and degree classification, the residency requirement will vary. For many of these degrees, ATS requires a minimum of one-third of the program to be done in residency or at an authorized extension site. For some of these degrees, a minimum of two-thirds of the program is required to be completed in residency. These are minimum thresholds for residential course work, but accredited schools are free to require the entire program to be done through residential course work. Member schools are allowed to apply for exceptions to these standards, so potential applicants may see variations in the educational format requirements.

Many of these programs are permitted by ATS to accept a limited number of students who do not hold a bachelor's degree, but schools are not required to do so. Because there is limited space for accepting students without the bachelor's degree, applicants can experience delays in the admissions and enrollment process.

Similar to the MDiv degree, master's programs oriented toward a specialized ministry will include the three apprenticeships: cognitive, practical, and identity formation. Because these degrees are intended to support recipients in the practice of their specialized ministry, the programs are required to foster the spiritual growth and development of the students. With some variation, these degrees will also include supervised work in the field as part of the program where students can receive feedback and guidance from a qualified practitioner.

Programs Oriented toward General Theological Education

Master's degrees in this classification are designed to provide participants with a broad exposure to theology and its subdisciplines. In the world of theological schools, they are often referred to as academic degrees, as opposed to the professional degrees named above. These degrees use the nomenclature of master of arts, master of arts (academic discipline, e.g., religion or theological studies), or master of theological studies. According to their classification, these degrees are not intended to prepare participants for the practice of ministry, even though the content of the degree could be beneficial to a practitioner.

Many theological schools offer at least one degree in this classification in addition to the more popular MDiv. Because the degree provides a general background in theology, graduates often use this degree to prepare for doctoral studies. In some cases people will pursue this degree to support an already established practice of ministry. Pastors who do not have a graduate degree in theology will sometimes pursue this degree instead of the MDiv. The degree is shorter by one year and therefore less expensive.

Because these degrees are not oriented toward a specific ministerial practice, there are significant differences in the content requirements and teaching formats. Each school is required to organize the degree around program goals and learning outcomes suited to the academic discipline being covered. Unlike the professional degrees, the academic degrees focus specifically on the cognitive apprenticeship and a limited amount on the practical apprenticeship, focusing particularly on skills needed for acceptable scholarship.

These degrees require a minimum of two years of study or its equivalent. However, ATS-accredited schools are permitted to offer the degree in a variety of formats: completely in residence, partially in residence and partially through distance education, or completely through distance education. The schools are required to demonstrate that the learning formats used achieve the educational experience outlined in the degree goals and learning outcomes.

These programs are not permitted to accept students who have not earned a baccalaureate degree.

Advanced Programs Oriented toward Theological Research and Teaching

The third classification of master's degrees in theology pertains to those degrees preparing participants for academic research and teaching. These degrees, like the ones pertaining to general theological education, are not designed to prepare people for the practice of ministry. Many of the participants in these degrees are either active lay leaders in congregations or ordained ministers, but they are engaging these degrees in pursuit of a position in theological scholarship. They are considered advanced degrees because students are trained to be more proficient in a particular aspect of theology. In many cases, students will seek one of these degrees after completing an MDiv or another master's degree in general theological study and before applying to a doctoral program.

Graduates of the programs are typically interested in teaching theology, either at the undergraduate or graduate level. Some will seek this type of degree in order to teach theology or religion in secondary education. The nomenclature used for these academic degrees includes master of theology and master of sacred theology.

The degrees that fall into this classification are created to give participants both a general knowledge of theology and exposure to a specialized subdiscipline of theology. Language studies, classical and/or modern, may be required, depending on the specialization.

These degrees require one year of full-time academic study or its equivalent. They also require the successful completion of an MDiv or its equivalent. Unless the school has petitioned for an exception, accredited-degree programs in this classification are required to be entirely residential. These programs are not permitted to be offered online.

TEACHING AND LEARNING FORMATS
OF THEOLOGICAL DEGREES

As noted throughout the degree descriptions and standards, theological degrees are taught in a variety of formats. Theological schools that are members in the Association of Theological Schools have agreed on common standards regarding the formats that can be utilized. Member schools are bound to follow these standards, which are considered to be the best practices for the teaching and learning of theology. ATS does have provisions for exceptions to the standards, but they are exceptions. When comparing programs for different schools, it is likely that an inquirer will see a lot of similarities and some variations.

Standards regarding distance education are based on the common wisdom of member schools. They are not arbitrary, even though they evolve over time. Some courses of study require what ATS documents refer to as "a comprehensive community of learning."[4] This language is meant to indicate that certain types of theological education require a variety of interactions between and among students and faculty members. The formation of ministerial leadership is larger than what happens in a classroom. Interactions in the dining room, gym, chapel, library, parking lot, hallways, communal spaces, classrooms, faculty offices, and supervised-ministry sites all contribute to the theological formation of the whole person. The obligation for ATS schools is to discern continually how a specific degree's goals and learning outcomes are best achieved.

Each discipline in higher education has a way of talking about the different teaching formats. Before you consider what the best program is for you, it is important to review the common nomenclature currently used in theological schools. The classification of courses is important, because it can obscure as much as it reveals about how a school constructs its courses and programs.

Distance Education. This is the general term for education in which the students and the faculty are not located in the same physical space for class. Course participants interact through online technologies, either at the same time (synchronously) or when the course participant chooses (asynchronously). Depending on the type, courses may include a limited amount of class time in the same physical space. See discussion later in this chapter.

Online Courses. An online course is a form of distance education. The course could be offered completely online or might include some interactions for students and faculty to be in the same physical space. For ATS schools, courses are classified as online courses if more than 50 percent of the course is completed online. Consequently, some courses that are described as online may not be completely accomplished online.

Residential Courses. In a residential course, the students and faculty are in the same physical space for class. They are commonly referred to as face-to-face courses. However, for ATS schools a course is classified as residential if more than 50 percent of the course is completed in the physical classroom. This means that courses considered residential could include up to 49 percent of online work for the course.

Hybrid Courses. A hybrid course involves the use of a physical classroom and an online classroom. The amount of time that the students and faculty spend in the same location is not prescribed for hybrid courses. Some hybrid courses alternate face-to-face sessions with online activities. Others begin and end the course with face-to-face sessions, filling in the middle with all online activities. Seminaries will often label a class as hybrid to indicate simply that the course will involve a mixture of learning formats. For accreditation purposes, however, courses are classified as either residential or online, depending on the balance of formats. Students wanting to know the residential requirements for a hybrid course should contact the registrar of the school.

Technology is now part of daily life. People post videos, share pictures, and communicate with loved ones online. Global telecommunication companies are continually creating new ways of sharing information, developing community, and learning skills through online tools. Theological education has increasingly embraced forms of online education. Most schools have incorporated online elements to their programs. Students submit papers and projects online, and faculty use the comment feature to give students feedback. Online classrooms document intense student debates that can allow more voices to be heard, including the voice of the most introverted student. Regardless of the program you choose, technology and online engagement should be assumed. The only question that remains is how much of it is appropriate for you.

TYPES OF THEOLOGICAL SCHOOLS

There are several typologies used to categorize theological schools. In most cases the distinctions are significant and have direct impact on a student's learning experience and future job prospects. Looking at the various options is integral to the discernment process.

Stand-Alone Schools and Embedded Schools

Some theological schools are part of a larger educational institution, either a college or university. Sometimes the theology school created the undergraduate program to complement the graduate program. In other cases the graduate program followed the creation of the undergraduate program. Either way, these schools are classified as embedded schools. The theology school and the larger institution can share resources, including dormitories, faculty, libraries, fitness facilities, and dining rooms. Embedded schools, in general, have more resources that allow them to have larger faculties and to offer a larger variety of theology degrees. Because embedded theology schools are part of a larger institution, they have to also abide by the rules of the wider campus. For example, rules regarding admission of graduate students would be affected by this association.

Stand-alone schools are not associated or under the governance of a college or university. They are freestanding. Stand-alone schools are often smaller, allowing for a more intimate learning experience. In these schools, faculty, staff, and students are more likely to know each other better. Some of the oldest theological schools in the country are stand-alone schools.

Both stand-alone and embedded schools can be associated with a particular denomination. The degree to which that association impacts the theology program varies significantly. Some denominational affiliations result in a strong ecumenical atmosphere. Others result in a very denominationally focused environment.

Theological Seminaries, Seminaries, Schools of Theology, and Divinity Schools

While there is some consistency in the nomenclature of theological schools, there remain exceptions in every category.

Generally, institutions that use the words *theological seminary* or *seminary* in their name are often stand-alone schools that focus the majority of their attention on preparing people for general and specialized forms of pastoral ministry. They are professional graduate schools. Many theological seminaries also offer academic and research degrees, employ research-focused faculty, and support research libraries on their campus.

Institutions that use *school* in their name are typically embedded schools. In many cases the university contains a series of schools, for example, the School of Nursing, the School of Theology, and the School of Law, or the university could have a Law School, a Medical School, and a Divinity School. These theological schools will offer both professional and academic degrees, preparing people for ministerial practice, theological research and teaching, or both. These schools will offer more research-oriented courses, employ research-focused faculty, and cultivate research libraries to support both.

Because there are exceptions in all these categories, sometimes significant exceptions, it's vital to look beyond the name of a school and find out about the ethos of the school in regard to how they envision the preparation of ministerial leaders and those interested in academic research and teaching. What does the school think is the best way to prepare for pastoral ministry? What kind of research does the school support? Where the school lands in relationship to these questions is more helpful to the discernment process than their name.

Denominational Affiliation, Theological Affiliation, Ecumenical, Nondenominational, and Interdenominational

For most people looking at a theological degree, how a school classifies itself in this way will play a significant role in the discernment process. In some cases, the denominational affiliation of someone looking toward ordained pastoral ministry will invoke clear restrictions on potential schools. For example, Roman Catholic men looking to be ordained Roman Catholic priests are allowed to attend only Roman Catholic schools. Roman Catholic seminarians are permitted to take courses at other seminaries, but they must complete their degrees at a Roman Catholic school.

Denominational affiliation is the most common way a theological school classifies its affiliation. Mennonite, Roman Catholic, United Methodist, Presbyterian, Episcopal, Disciples of Christ, United Church of Christ, Church of the Brethren, Unitarian Universalist, Orthodox, Baptist, and African Methodist Episcopal are some examples of the denominational affiliations of theological schools. With a few exceptions, most denominationally affiliated schools will take students from any denomination. In fact, many schools that are affiliated with a particular denomination are quick to demonstrate that they are also ecumenical.

Theological affiliation is a way that some schools want to communicate their adherence to a particular strand of or perspective within Christianity. For example, a school may describe itself as biblical, Evangelical, or Pentecostal. Because these affiliations cross denominational lines, some of these schools also call themselves nondenominational or multidenominational.

"Ecumenical" and "interdenominational" are labels that are used by schools in a variety of ways, all invoking the sense that the school pertains to more than the interests of just one denomination. Many schools will use either term to describe themselves as a way to communicate that the faculty and student body include people from a variety of denominations. Some schools will use the term "ecumenical," claiming that the school promotes or supports the whole of Christianity. Sometimes the label "ecumenical" is used in conjunction with a denominational affiliation for the school, other times not. As we will explore in the following chapter, the words "ecumenical" and "interdenominational" can hide as much as they reveal about a school.

Applicants with a strong theological or denominational attachment will want to inquire about how others like themselves have fared at the school. No school has the resources or the space in the curriculum to teach all theological opinions and traditions. Some perspectives will get more air time in the classroom. The question at this point is, how does a school articulate its commitments to the breadth of Christianity, and what does its version of ecumenism or interdenominationalism look like, in detail?

As is the case with other professions, there are numerous ways in which one can pursue pastoral ministry and a theological education. Knowing the different kinds of schools, the kind of degrees available, and the possible learning formats that could be used to obtain a theology degree are all essential to the discernment process. In the next chapter we'll discuss what to consider when deciding whether to pursue a theological education. There is more to it than selecting a school and degree program.

3

Discerning and Deciding

"Beside the degree, school, and teaching format, what are the other things that I need to think about if I am interested in theological studies?" "What is the process for making a decision?" "What do I need to do?" These are the questions that I regularly hear in my work as a seminary professor and administrator. And they are the right questions to be asking. In chapter 1 I introduced the practices of discernment and making choices, which are elemental to wise living. In chapter 2 we looked at the variety of degree programs, schools, and teaching/ learning formats that are available. There are, however, more areas of discernment to consider before making a decision. In this chapter we'll walk through each of them and then conclude with making your decision.

I have put the following considerations in the order that I think best facilitates the discernment process. In the end, it will still require holding all of them together when it comes time to make your decision.

AREAS OF DISCERNMENT

Vocational Trajectory

If you are still reading this book, I am assuming that you continue to be interested in theological education and the possibility of seeking a degree. The question remains, what do you hope to do with the degree? How you answer this question, in combination with your denominational affiliation, will likely be the biggest factors in your discernment process.

While some readers are already sure about pursuing a degree to support some form of authorized ministry, it's worth the time to explore this point explicitly. Even those who are already authorized for ministry will benefit from exploring how their vocational path influences this decision.

As a way to explore your vocational options, I suggest you do the exercise below. I call it the mission-and-mandate exercise.

Research the mission and mandates of your denomination or anticipated area of future work. Research may include consulting ministry handbooks, official denominational publications, ordination rites, and representatives of the field. Be sure to research implicit and explicit expectations. You should be knowledgeable about the requirements of your intended vocation and be able to explain them to others.

Here are questions to consider as you do your research:

— What is the stated mission of your denomination or religious community? Or what is the stated mission of your intended vocational area? For example, if you are thinking about being a Presbyterian pastor, what is the stated mission of the Presbyterian Church? If you are interested in becoming a college chaplain, research some of the published mission statements of college chaplaincies. If you aren't sure of your vocational area, use this exercise to check out different options.

— What is the mandate, charge, or expectation for those wishing to be an authorized leader in that religious community or for those being certified in that field? There should be a clear connection between the mission of the institution and the mandate for those certified or authorized to be representatives.

— What are the levels or types of authorization? Examples include federal certification, ordination, board certification, and being commissioned.

— What are the explicit (named) requirements of your intended vocation within that institution? Include both preparatory and ongoing requirements. For example, "successful candidates for

ordination in this fellowship must complete one unit of clinical pastoral education (CPE)."
—What are the implicit (implied but not necessarily discussed) requirements? Include both preparatory and ongoing requirements. For example, "successful candidates for ordination in this denomination must be willing to plant churches in countries outside the United States."

The mission-and-mandate exercise is intended to get you thinking about what is required of a person for a particular vocation. By requirements I mean degrees and training, but I also mean more than that. Some vocations, depending on their context, can have very specific requirements. For example, some denominations will not ordain women. Some will ordain only celibate men. Others will not support a divorced person in ministry. Other types of requirements include commitments to doctrinal fidelity, daily prayer, social action, and institutional obedience.

The exercise is also important because it helps us understand more clearly that there are implicit and explicit expectations for every vocation. If we haven't done our research or haven't spoken with someone who is engaged in that vocation, we won't know the unspoken expectations that are placed on people. If pursuing ordination includes celibacy, for instance, that's an important detail to know up front.

In addition to understanding the requirements of a particular vocation, this exercise helps to draw out your own commitments, values, and priorities so that you can see them in relationship to the vocation and context you are imagining. If you are thinking about becoming an authorized minister of a denomination, it would be an important point of discernment to know that you are in tension with the denomination over a central doctrine. It doesn't automatically mean that you should no longer think about ministry in that context, but it does suggest that you need to give attention to that reality in your considerations.

Denominational Affiliation

Denominational affiliation and the extent to which you are affiliated with a denomination can have an extensive impact on your vocational path and education. If you are interested in pursuing authorized ministry, your denominational affiliation will impact funding, theological school, degree program, and course requirements.

Most, if not all, denominations prefer that you begin the discernment process with the local church and its leadership before applying to a theological school. Some denominations will require preauthorization before you can apply to a seminary. That preauthorization includes acceptance in the official clergy discernment process of that denomination and would come from a regional or centralized office. It varies by denomination.[1] The best way to begin your research about the process that your denomination follows is to ask your pastor or another authorized minister within the denomination. When you do the mission-and-mandate exercise outlined above, you'll have a good idea of what is expected.

Here are a few things you should know. If you belong to a Roman Catholic, Orthodox, or Episcopal Church[2] and hope to pursue ordination in that denomination, you will be expected to attend a seminary determined by the bishop. Some bishops will be open to suggestions from a candidate, but many will not consult with you about which school you should attend. In these traditions it is not appropriate for you to tell the bishop where you plan to attend seminary and which degree program you plan to pursue. In addition, you will need acceptance into the denominational discernment process before you'll be authorized to apply to a seminary.

If you are a member of a Protestant church that isn't Episcopal, you will likely have more options regarding schools. These denominations typically operate their own seminaries but will allow clergy candidates to attend seminaries that are not associated with the denomination. Each denomination is different in regard to which other seminaries are acceptable. While you have more options than the first group, it is still wise to talk with an authorized minister in the denomination and the denominational office for clergy candidates before applying to a program.

If you are a member of denomination identified as Evangelical or Pentecostal, you too will likely have options regarding which theological school you can attend. As noted in chapter 2, there are schools that identify as Evangelical or Pentecostal. Sometimes they are associated with a denomination, but more often they will describe themselves as interdenominational, multidenominational, or nondenominational. In these cases it is considered best practice, as it is with the other Protestant traditions, to contact your local pastor and a denominational office before proceeding with a seminary application.

Taking your denominational affiliation seriously is one of the first steps toward pursuing authorized or ordained ministry in that community. There is a temptation to see the entire discernment process as a matter between God and ourselves. But it's much more communal, as we'll see in the next section.

Listening and Watching for God

What is God's will for my life? In my experience, this is how many people situate their vocational discernment process. When I decided to apply to seminary, I wanted to be a priest. I asked a trusted English teacher to help me with my application essay. When he asked me why I wanted to be ordained, he didn't wait for me to formulate a reply. Instead he said, "There is only one reason to seek ordination: because God wants you to be a minister."

I have reflected on my teacher's assessment of the discernment process many times over the years. On the one hand, his perspective was helpful to me, because it helped me to know, right from the beginning, that the process couldn't be reduced to my deciding what I wanted to do with my life. At that point in the process I was focused on naming what I wanted to do. That wasn't a bad thing; it was just incomplete.

On the other hand, my teacher's comments had a negative impact on me and my discernment process. Because he stated that God's will was the only reason for seeking ordination, he didn't leave any room for my hopes and desires or for the expressed interests of my faith community. As he framed the discernment process, my choice was only a matter of doing God's will or not doing God's will. The truth was that I had no idea what God wanted or how to assess what God wanted. I also didn't know a lot about my own desires; I was simply too young and naive.

"What is God's will for my life?" This is not the most helpful question to be asking at this stage of the discernment process. The question is too theologically complex. In fact, most of us can barely state what *our will* is for our life. Most of us don't know ourselves deeply enough to make that assessment.

Instead, I would suggest using the language and questions commonly used by those who do spiritual guidance:[3] "What is God's invitation to me?" "What is the grace that I am being offered with this invitation?"

Although still challenging, these questions will serve as better guides in the discernment process. The language of invitation makes space for us to make our own response to God's initiative. It means that the end result grows out of our working together with God. It requires us to listen for and pay attention to God's invitation, and it requires us to claim our own voice in the process. To speak of God's invitation to us doesn't preclude God from having a will, but it does open the space for both ourselves and God to have wills and desires.

God's invitations and graces can come to us in many ways. We may be inspired as we reflect on a Bible passage, sing a hymn, listen to a sermon, serve a stranger, hike in a forest, or hear a testimony of grace. Maybe people seek us out for spiritual counsel; they experience us as a thoughtful or prayerful person. Perhaps we are inspired by the example of another person making a sacrifice on behalf of others. We can talk to God in prayer about our lives and what we should do with our lives. We should. God's responses, however, rarely come in the form of a direct response to a question. Instead they come through interactions that include the world. God points our attention to the condition of the world, invites us to consider the possibilities God has for it, and waits for us to return with our response.

Simply put, God's role in our discernment can't be limited to a specific point in our process. We don't simply begin or end by asking God to share with us what we are supposed to do. God is present in the invitation, our personal history, our deepest yearnings, the longing of the world, the people in our lives. When we hold all those things before God and with God, God is present in the holding. God's invitation to us emerges when we make the more fundamental decision to be a disciple and to join God in beholding the world anew. Your denomination and theological school will join you in listening for God's invitation to you. They will also pay attention for the graces that will come with the invitation.

WHO DECIDES WHAT

The ordination of a minister within a particular denomination is the culmination of a process in which all the deciding parties agree that the person presented for authorization is fit for general ministry throughout the denomination. One of the responsibilities of an ordained clergy person is to represent the entire denomination, both within and outside the denomination.[4] Consequently, the approval process goes beyond what any individual wishes, including the person seeking approval. In every denomination there are multiple stages of input and levels of decision making as a seminarian moves through the formation process. Even when the ultimate decision to ordain a willing clergy candidate rests with a bishop, many other people are consulted in the process. Those consultants have significant impact on the final decision.

Your Role

If you don't belong to a denomination or religious community that requires preauthorization or acceptance into a clergy candidate program before applying to seminary or if you aren't interested in authorized ministry of any kind, the decision to apply to a theological school is up to you. You can apply to a degree program even if you don't know what you want to do with the degree, as long as the school is willing to accept you without authorization from the denomination. One word of caution: if you decide to pursue ordination with a denomination or religious community after having already begun a degree program or completed one, the ordaining body may still impose additional requirements or courses of study. Communities that ordain or authorize ministers want to be involved in the educational process of clergy candidates as it happens. Because the discernment process is communal, their voice matters. Don't assume that you can get authorization for ministry just because you have the right degree and believe that you are called by God.

The Denomination's Role

As we have noted above, some denominations will not permit you to attend seminary or support a person in a seminary program until the person has been preapproved to be a seminarian. Roman Catholic seminaries fall into this category.[5] Once you are approved to be a seminarian, the bishop will tell you the seminary where you are to apply. The Episcopal and Orthodox denominations proceed in a similar fashion. Most Protestant denominations keep the process of acceptance into an ordination track separate from the process of applying to a seminary. While they typically prefer you to engage their approval process *before* applying to seminary, once you are approved, there is significant freedom about which school you can attend. The nomenclature for being accepted into the official discernment and preparation process of a denomination varies. "Candidate," "in care," "inquirer," and "novice" are some of the terms used by denominations. Some denominations will have a series of stages and corresponding titles for the seminarian at each point.

The Theological School's Role

Each school has its own independent application process, even if it is associated with a denomination. For example, a United Methodist person may be accepted into candidacy (the official term for the period of discernment and preparation for ministry), but that does not guarantee acceptance into a seminary, including a United Methodist school. That being said, theological schools do work closely with denominations regarding qualifications for authorized ministry. The schools and the denominations share a commitment to preparing leaders for the church and world. Some schools will regularly invite denominational officials to participate in the midprogram review of seminarians.

Just as acceptance into the ministry preparation process by a denomination doesn't guarantee acceptance into a degree program, the reverse is also true. Acceptance into a degree program doesn't mean that a denomination will offer its official endorsement of a seminarian. Some schools do require official denominational approval, either for acceptance into a degree program or within the first year of studies. Many schools, however, are willing to accept people who are not authorized by their denomination to attend seminary.

In some cases, the seminary is all too eager to accept an applicant because it needs students. As an applicant, it's your responsibility to know how much input your denomination will require in the educational process. You cannot assign that responsibility to the school, and the school cannot claim to speak for the denomination either. Each party has a distinct role to play in the process.

PERTINENT DEGREE(S)

In chapter 2 we reviewed the various theological degree categories and the basic trajectories and requirements for those degree programs. In terms of the discernment process, here are a few things that you need to consider before identifying the right degree for you.

If you know the general vocational path that you intend to pursue and you know the requirements of your denomination or intended ministry, selecting a degree program isn't too complicated. For example, those interested in becoming an ordained pastor of a church should be looking at the master of divinity degree, unless your denomination allows you to undertake a two-year master's program. (If they do allow clergy candidates to do a general two-year theological degree, you'll have more options from which to choose.)

There are certain ministerial paths and some denominations that require a bachelor's degree and a master's degree. In a few cases, a denomination will require a specific amount of philosophy or another discipline at the bachelor's level before allowing a candidate to proceed to graduate studies. Board certification with the Association of Professional Chaplains currently requires both a bachelor's degree and a graduate-level theology degree with at least seventy-two credit hours.

If you have an unclear sense of your vocational path but want to begin theological studies, you have a couple of choices. You can select the degree that has the most flexibility for future application, or you can apply to be an unclassified student. Most schools will allow qualified applicants to take three to five courses without applying to a specific degree program. These students are considered unclassified. This approach allows the student to get a taste of theological studies without committing to a particular degree and vocational path. If you decide to apply to a degree program after a few courses and you are accepted, most schools will count any successfully completed courses toward your degree. If you decide to begin as an unclassified student, you won't be eligible for any federal loan program. You are also unlikely to receive any type of scholarship funding, which means that you'll need to pay the tuition out of pocket.

FULL-TIME OR PART-TIME

Most theological schools accept both full-time and part-time students. The Roman Catholic and Orthodox schools are the exception. Those schools are organized as residential programs that require students to go full-time and to live on campus.

Each institution is responsible for determining how many credits constitute full-time and part-time loads. Generally, twelve semester credits or more is considered full-time; anything less than twelve semester credits is considered part-time. However, in order to qualify for federal student loans, a student must take at least six credits during each academic period.

If you are looking at a program that is partially or completely offered online, it could be tempting to ignore the difference between going full-time or part-time. Taking courses online is just as rigorous as taking them on campus. For some people online courses are more difficult. Online courses require more than introductory technology skills. They require digital literacy and the ability to troubleshoot computer issues. If because of your other commitments you don't have the time and space to be a full-time student on campus, you will most likely not be able to do full-time studies online either.

There are several major factors to consider when deciding whether you should go full-time or part-time: family commitments, work commitments, the quality of education, and finances.

Family Commitments

Students who have family responsibilities need to take those into account when determining whether it is feasible to go full-time. Twelve semester credits entail a significant amount of work, beyond what is expected in most bachelor's programs. Students should expect a minimum of a thousand pages of reading for each three-credit course.

Responsibilities for children, parents, spouses, and other family members need to be acknowledged when considering your options. Whether you go part-time or full-time, family responsibilities will need to be adjusted. You'll have less time to devote to typical household chores. We'll come back to this in the next section of the book, but it's important to note now that you'll need to make changes in your daily life. The fewer responsibilities you have for family members, the more realistic it is to be a full-time student.

Work Commitments

Your work commitments, like your family commitments, will have a direct impact on how many credits you'll be able to take at one time. If you intend to work full-time during your theological studies, it's not advisable to enroll as a full-time student. A seminary may incentivize students to go full-time by offering extra financial aid, but it's critical that a student realistically assess how much she or he will need to complete course requirements. Furthermore, if you have family commitments and work commitments, your wisest and only realistic option is to enroll as a part-time student.

Impact on Quality of Education

It's now possible to enroll as a part-time theology student and to receive a quality education. You will likely not benefit from some of the communal and social elements of a full-time, residential program, but you can have a rich educational experience and achieve a theological degree. If you are intending to be a part-time student, you'll need to strategically determine how to take full advantage of all the resources that a school has to offer.

The unfortunate reality is that not all schools are equally prepared to serve part-time students. While most schools are willing to accept part-time students, many of them have not created an entire degree around the needs of part-time students. Most schools have taken the full-time program and arranged to offer it at alternative times and locations. Many schools now offer courses online or in the evening. Offering courses at different times is not the same as having a complete program for part-time students. Consequently, there is often a negative impact for the part-time student.

If you need to be a part-time student, investigate how these things are handled or made available: faculty advising, chapel services, commuter gathering spaces, commuter dormitories, library hours, online library services, and student socials. Not all these items will be equally important to everyone, but you should understand whether a school has a program for part-time students or just tolerates part-time students. If it's the latter, then you may need to make more adjustments in your life to accommodate what the school has to offer.

Finances

We'll talk about financing your education in several places throughout the book. For the moment, we'll focus on how going part-time or full-time impacts the finances of your graduate degree. There are two key points to consider.

The first issue is that most schools have more scholarship funding available for full-time students than part-time students. In some cases, the scholarship funds are restricted by the guidelines that were established when the endowments were created. A school can't violate those agreements. Also, from a financial perspective, schools prefer to enroll full-time students. Full-time students use less of a school's resources. Hence, more scholarship funding is devoted to full-time students. Many denominations also have scholarship funding available. Often more funds are designated for full-time students, because the denomination or institution wants to incentivize doing full-time studies.

The second issue revolves around whether you intend to use federal loans to underwrite your education. If you plan to take advantage of these loans, consider how many years it will take you to complete the degree. Federal guidelines require that you take at least six semester credits during the academic period to qualify for student loans, which means that you can still receive federal loans while going to school part-time. If the degree takes you six years to complete the requirements going part-time, you could be eligible for six years of student loans. That is helpful when you are taking classes, but your student debt amount escalates with every year in the program. The final loan amount will increase even more if you take out the maximum amount allowed each year. So if you are going to use federal loans to support your part-time studies, it is wise to take the smallest amount possible. I am not suggesting that you should use credit cards or bank loans as alternatives to the federal loan program. Those options can have worse consequences. The goal is to rely as little as possible on borrowed funding, from any source. Working early and closely with the student loan officer of a school is critical to successfully funding your education and sustaining healthy finances.[6]

TEACHING AND LEARNING FORMAT

As we noted in chapter 2, theological schools are experimenting and innovating when it comes to offering theological education. Right now the main program options range from completely online programs to completely residential programs. Some schools and some denominations don't support online teaching and learning. Some denominations, such as The United Methodist Church, restrict which schools you can use for online classes. Be sure to check with your denomination if you intend to use your degree for an authorized ministry position.

The educational philosophy of the school, the strength of the program, and technical matters are the key points of consideration when it comes to assessing which learning format is best for you.

Educational Philosophy of the School

Most schools do not have an explicitly stated educational philosophy, so it can be difficult to assess how each school understands the process of learning and teaching. An articulated educational philosophy would cover a number of areas in the teaching and learning process. The key issue here related to the teaching and learning format is the extent to which a school understands education as the transferal of data or information from the teacher to the students. Paolo Freire coined the term "banking education" to describe what happens when education is understood as a teacher depositing information in the minds of students.[7] When learning is understood this way, students are expected to memorize and repeat what they heard from the professor.

An alternative to this model is to see the educational endeavor as awakening the students' minds so that they can participate in the intellectual work together with the professor. In this alternative philosophy, the students are understood as original and critical thinkers, actors, and subjects alongside the professor, not reduced to passive, oppressed receptors of ideas. Students do need to engage information and data transmitted by the professor. The debate is over *how* that information is engaged and *to what purpose.*

I raise the educational philosophy of the school in this context because debates over the value of online versus residential education are often lightly veiled arguments about the value of the banking model of education. Some critics of online education suggest that it reinforces the banking model. It may be true that web-based activities provide a helpful context to review and repeat important pieces of information, thus making online education vulnerable to the banking model. But many residential programs, despite the time and space they have to focus on active learning, continue to rely on teaching techniques, such as lecture-based courses, that promote the banking perspective. The fact that a program is online doesn't mean that it seeks to maintain the oppression of the students through required regurgitation of information. In addition, the fact that a program is residential doesn't guarantee that it uses education to activate and liberate the minds and lives of students.

When looking at different schools, it's not enough to look at whether the program is online, hybrid, or residential. The educational philosophy of the school is what will shape your learning experience. Because it can be so challenging to find out what the educational philosophy of a school is, talk with current students and recent graduates and review some of the syllabi of the required courses. From that information you can get a good idea about how the development and expansion of your mind and life will be addressed in the program.

Program Strength

A well-rounded and impactful degree program requires more than a collection of courses. Seminary students need advising and quality time with other seminarians. The interactions that occur outside the official classroom are often where significant integration, spiritual formation, and personal growth happen. That doesn't mean that a well-rounded program can be accomplished only in a residential model. Some schools are devoting significant resources to designing complete online programs, which will include spiritual formation. It's important to investigate whether a school is offering a well-rounded program or whether the degree is simply a matter of taking the prescribed courses and number of credits. In schools that have not implemented a complete and holistic program, students will struggle to stay engaged with their studies and their peers. They will drift away. Schools that have clear and strong programs help students integrate their learning along the way, connect with peers, and deepen their investment in the purpose of the degree.

Technical Matters

Nearly all schools today will require at least some online work and web-based interactions. Some technical skills will be required for any program. You'll be expected to upload papers, photographs, videos, and other materials. You'll also need to know how to contribute to online discussions, create and edit team web documents, research online catalogs, and participate in live web events.

If you find that your technical skills are not sufficient, it would be worth taking a computer course or workshop that would bring you to a higher level of proficiency. If a school, program, or course has technical requirements, you'll need to comply with them. Schools that utilize web-based learning and teaching will have published hardware, software, and skill requirements. The more online work a school requires, the greater these requirements will be. Because online and hybrid courses require computer hardware, software, and technical skills, it's important to assess whether you and the school are ready to support this type of educational experience.

In addition to assessing your own technical skills and compatibility with online learning, inquire about what technical support the school offers for students and classes. Support systems vary greatly from school to school, so do not assume what is available. For example, if you experience technical difficulties with an online classroom at eleven o'clock in the evening, is there tech support available at that hour? Or is it available only during school business hours? The more tech savvy you are, the less dependent you'll be on tech support from the school.

RACE, GENDER, CLASS, SEXUAL ORIENTATION

Just as the United States is becoming more diverse each year, Christianity and its theological schools in the United States are also becoming more diverse. African American, Latino/a American, and Asian American students are the fastest growing populations in theological schools. This changing reality has become a catalyst for acknowledging and addressing long-standing issues related to race, gender, class, and sexual orientation in theology and theological education. Among the questions I think are important to your discernment process are these:

— To what extent does a school include matters of race, gender, class, economic status, and sexual orientation as an explicit part of the educational experience and curriculum?

— To what extent are privilege and supremacy in regards to race, gender, class, economic status, and sexual orientation openly addressed in courses and the wider curriculum?

— To what extent does a school expose students to the diversity of humanity and cultivate an appreciation for the wisdom that is provided through that diversity?

When you are looking at particular schools, these questions can get you started. Getting answers to these questions can be challenging. Here are a few things you can do to explore the extent to which a school is engaged with these realities.

Diversity of Student Body, Faculty, Staff, and Trustees

The compositions of the student body, faculty, staff, and trustees are often posted by a seminary on their website. If not, you can ask the director of admissions for this information. There is no magic number that you should be looking for in a school. Instead, look at the extent to which there is diversity within the various groups. To what extent are African Americans, Asian Americans, and Latino/a Americans represented in the community? How about people who are gay, lesbian, bisexual, or transgender? Does the school accept women into all degree programs? Diversity in every category may not be present in a particular school, given its physical location, theological commitments, or ecclesiastical rules. If you have a choice in what seminary you will attend, understanding the extent to which the community is diverse should be a factor in your discernment. The more diverse the community is, the more opportunities you'll have to learn from people who are different from yourself. If you are required to attend a school that is not particularly diverse, it would enhance your education if you pursued as many opportunities as possible to engage with people who are different from you.

Privilege and Supremacy

Privilege and supremacy are not the same things. Privilege is a matter of one particular group of people having more access to resources than other groups. Supremacy is a matter of believing that one particular group is better than another or more worthwhile than another. These two are often confused because they typically occur together. If a person, group, or institution thinks that one group is more valuable than the others (supremacy), he, she, or it will then provide more advantages to the members of the more "valuable" group (privilege). Issues of privilege and supremacy have been at the center of American life since the nation's inception. Consequently, they are also embedded in our theological institutions and our theologies. I'm not sure that there exists a school that addresses these realities perfectly. We have been miseducating ourselves for a long time, and it will take a long time to correct our educational system when it comes to issues of supremacy and privilege.

Every theological school in America should discuss and wrestle with supremacy in all its forms and the privilege each form brings, including white supremacy, heterosexual supremacy, male supremacy, and wealth supremacy. Look at a seminary's website for evidence that demonstrates its commitment to wrestling with these issues. Ask current students, recent graduates, and professors about what they are learning through their attentiveness to these topics. If they are actively engaged in the conversation, they will have something to share.

Respect for Diversity of Knowledge Sources

If you want to explore how diversity is handled in the classroom, talk with the professors or ask to see a few example syllabi from required courses. I look for two things when I am trying to assess how diversity may be handled in a particular course: the reading list and the course assignments. Does the reading list include a diversity of perspectives on the course topic? You may not recognize any of the authors' names and may need to look them up online. When the required reading list includes a variety of backgrounds, it suggests that the professor is committed to listening to multiple voices.

The course assignments are another place where the values of the course are clearly demonstrated, because they have been designed by the professor to assess what a student has learned. That is to say, course assignments reflect the priorities of the professor in regard to the course topic. The questions are: does the course assess all students on the many available perspectives pertinent in the field? Is everybody required to demonstrate an understanding of an African American author included on the reading list? Or does the course give students *the option* to research African American theologizing, feminist theologizing, or queer theologizing for a given assignment? Assignments that give students the option to explore particular voices within a theological discipline do not by themselves foster a common respect for the wisdom that comes from these communities. Instead, such assignments suggest that what these communities have to offer is optional or pertains only to those who belong to that community. When not everyone is expected to read and understand theologizing done by African Americans, feminists, or LGBT theologians, their work is not considered a crucial part of the Christian tradition.

Campus Housing

Housing at seminaries and divinity schools has changed significantly over the past few decades. Some schools have modern apartments that will support a small family. Some have traditional dormitories where students share bathroom facilities and common living areas. Many schools have created commuter housing for those who come to campus for one or more days each week. Even if you have no desire or intention to relocate, it's worth taking a look at what each school offers. While much of the housing that is available at theological schools isn't elegant, it is usually less expensive than what you can find in the surrounding area. If you don't own your own home, you may be able to reduce your housing and commuter expenses significantly if you move into campus housing. You should also check with the admissions office if there are any scholarships that assist with housing expenses. If there are, they will typically support on-campus housing only.

There are other reasons to live on campus apart from the reduction in housing and commuting expenses. Theological education programs foster a strong sense of community among the students. Instead of spending time traveling, students spend more time together. Potluck dinners, prayer services, movie nights, and parties are just a few of the events you are likely to enjoy if you live on campus. These informal moments allow you to know each other better and help you to know yourself better. They may not be part of the official curriculum, but they can be influential to your spiritual formation. The friends that you make in seminary are likely to last a lifetime.

MAKING YOUR DECISIONS

Elizabeth Liebert, in her book *The Way of Discernment*, proposes that there are several foundations that support the practice of discernment as one approaches a decision. Two of those foundations are particularly relevant as you discern and make a decision about taking on formal theological education.[8] Once you can embrace these two foundations, you'll be prepared to address the questions and decisions before you.

Foundation One

The first foundation is the importance of desire. Liebert makes clear just how crucial our desires are to the process when she writes, "In discernment, desires are the royal road to self-knowledge."[9] The premise is that God is at work in our desires. They are the path that leads us to our deepest self and to how God is at work in our lives. The challenge is that we don't always know what we desire, and sometimes we have to push ourselves to look beneath how we express our desires to find what we truly seek.

As you approach your decision of whether or not to apply to seminary, you have an opportunity to explore your desires and how God may be working in them. Some of you may be more aware of your desires. Even so, Liebert's exercise can help you take a deeper look at what is at work in your desire for ministry and a theological education. What is it that you seek? Who is it that you yearn for?

Liebert offers a prayer exercise to help you identify your desires. I have adapted it for vocational discernment. She suggests that during a period of extended prayer, where you have asked the Holy Spirit to guide your reflections, you write down on a piece of paper your answer to this question: "What do I want, right this minute?" You are to continue writing down answers to this question until you no longer have any additional responses.

Once you have the list of what you want, Liebert instructs you to identify the items on the list that are most pertinent to your current process and take them into the next step of prayer time. What desires emerged for you in the first step that are related to studying theology or pursuing ministry? In this second step, ask yourself, without judging the desire or yourself, "What is underneath this desire that I named? What desire is even more basic than this one?"

After you have done this second step with each of your original, pertinent stated desires, you begin to see what yearnings and needs are at work on a deeper level. You may need to repeat this second step with what you have found, asking yourself again, "What is underneath this deeper desire that I named? Is there something yet unnamed?"

Keep a journal about each step and the desires that you discover. You are not likely to discover what you really desire after only one session. In fact, you may need to repeat this exercise numerous times in order to find out what is at work in you on the deepest, most basic level. If you do this exercise on a regular basis, you'll discover how discernment can become a way of life, not something you do only when facing a decision. At the end of each prayer session, you are invited then to close the session by offering these desires back to God and giving thanks for the presence of the Spirit during this time of discernment.

Clarity of our deepest desires is the most fundamental piece of self-knowledge that we need when considering what we think God's invitation is to us. Once we have a sense of our deepest desires, we can assess the extent to which we want what God wants.

Foundation Two

The second foundation from Liebert's list is the spiritual freedom that comes through indifference. What she means by indifference is not a call to being careless, impartial, or lacking attachment. She writes, "Our first task of discernment, then, is to dispose ourselves to God's love, to become aware of God's presence, and then to frame our intention to follow God insofar as possible. This purity of intention is itself a gift of God. Our part is to sincerely *desire* it; God's part is to work it in us over time. Ignatius of Loyola chose a word for this purity of intention—indifference."[10]

The invitation, as Liebert understands it, is to become indifferent to anything that is not part of God's will so that we will focus our energy and lives on fulfilling God's will. In relationship to discerning an invitation to ministry and theological education, it's important to assess how free you are to respond and to choose. To what extent are you spiritually free to respond to God? Are you free from the coercion and the projected desires of others for your life? If you are not spiritually free, what do you need to do to become so?

Spiritual freedom is much harder to cultivate than we may imagine, because we live in a world where people and institutions are constantly trying to coerce us into acting in accordance with their best interests, disguised as our best interests. Innocence, security, fame, envy, and power are just a few enticements that we are offered in exchange for our cooperation, endorsement, and indifference.

In my experience, spiritual freedom that comes from indifference is the most challenging part of making discernment a part of regular life. Consequently, when it comes time to make significant life decisions, we are unprepared to assess the extent to which we are spiritually free.

Liebert offers another exercise for seeking spiritual freedom, which I have reworked for our purposes.

> Begin by asking the Holy Spirit to be with you as you seek to know God's will and invitation to you.
> Then, talk with God as you would talk with a friend. Reflect on the following statements in your time with God:
>
> — You created me, God, and knew me before I knew myself.
> — You desire that human beings flourish. You place in me a deep desire to abide in you and to flourish. Help me, God, to know what will allow me to flourish and thus fulfill your desire for me and for my life.
> — Even though I sometimes look to securing my own life, help me to desire what you desire and to see that as the path to my fulfillment and my best self.
>
> Thank God for God's presence in this time of prayer. Commit yourself to seeking God's desire for your life and to making it your desire. If you aren't there yet, ask God to give you the desire to desire what God wills. Wherever we are, we can ask God to meet us.
> Thank God for any clarity that you have received during this time of prayer. Thank God for the gift of spiritual freedom.

YOUR DECISIONS

If you have done the research, reflection, and prayer exercises suggested so far, you now have a significant amount of information to hold together. The truth is that you have several questions and decisions facing you at this point:

Questions	Decisions
Is God inviting you to some form of Christian ministry? What path will allow you to flourish as a human being? Are you free spiritually to respond to God's invitation?	How are you going to respond to that invitation?
Does the form of Christian ministry require a theological degree? If so, which degree?	Which degree do you intend to pursue?
Do you have any denominational, familial, logistical, or personal concerns that would impact the selection of theological schools where you would apply? If you have a denominational commitment that is pertinent, will you seek authorization with it to apply to a theological school?	To which theological schools will you apply?

As you pray and reflect over all the information that you have gathered, you may realize that ordained or authorized ministry is not your path, or at least not part of your path, right now. If so, that is important information, and the spiritual freedom that helped you to come to this realization will have hopefully given you greater clarity on your next steps.

If you have concluded that you are called to some form of authorized ministry which includes a theological degree, turn to chapter 4 to begin the process of applying to theological schools.

ADDITIONAL READING

Freire, Paolo. *Pedagogy of the Oppressed, 30th Anniversary Edition*. With an introduction by Ronaldo Macedo. Translated by Myra Bergman Ramos. New York: Bloomsbury, 2000.

hooks, bell. *Teaching Community: A Pedagogy of Hope*. New York: Routledge, 2003.

Liebert, Elizabeth. *The Way of Discernment: Spiritual Practices for Decision Making*. Louisville, KY: Westminster John Knox Press, 2008.

4

Learning What You Need to Know for Ministry

At the beginning of every semester in seminary I remember being filled with excitement. Deciding which courses I would take was always so challenging, because I was interested in all the topics. "How could I possibly choose between a theology course on grace and a Bible course on the book of Acts?" I would ask myself. But I did make choices. I had to make them. There were simply too many courses and not enough time. I did have one consolation. If I learned how to read theology books and to think theologically, I could continue my education long after my degree was completed. I didn't have to stop learning, ever.

I was also filled with trepidation, especially during the first two weeks of class. Once I had attended the first class session in all my courses for the semester, I would sit down and map out in my calendar all the assignment due dates. Having them posted together in one place helped me to keep track of what research I needed to be doing and when I needed to start writing. After I had written in all the deadlines, I would always, yes always, think to myself, "I'll never be able to get all this reading completed and all these papers written!" But I did get them done. Having a research and writing plan was the only way that I was able to do it.

As we discussed in chapter 2, preparation for most professional vocations includes three apprenticeships: cognitive, practical, and identity formation. In this chapter we will highlight important dimensions of your intellectual development and the cognitive apprenticeship. While it is helpful to interpret an entire degree program through these three apprenticeships, it's also important to remember that each apprenticeship requires you to integrate what you are learning with the other two apprenticeships. The three apprenticeships are not three distinct projects. They are three facets of the entirety of your education and formation as a minister or spiritual leader. We'll end this chapter talking about your work with your faculty adviser and how it can help you to see the interconnection of all the apprenticeships.

As its title indicates, the cognitive apprenticeship is the part of a theological education that addresses *what* you need to know and *how* you think. The two things go together because the information that you engage with in your courses will ultimately have an impact on how you think. They *won't determine* how you think, but the information will suggest patterns to you for considering information. There will be a lot of information that you will be expected to engage, debate, and remember. While professors realize that you will not retain all that information, they will expect the information to shape the way you approach similar theological issues. They also want you to know *where* to find the information that you need for ministry and *how* to reengage that information when it becomes important to do so.

Seminarians are sometimes surprised by how much information they are expected to learn during their degree program. I think that this happens for at least a couple of reasons. The first is that seminarians often think that preparation for authorized ministry is focused solely on a limited number of practical skills: preaching, providing pastoral care, and leading worship. Consequently, students can find it difficult to understand how studying the history of the early church would positively impact their pastoral practices. This is understandable, because they don't know what they don't know. If they haven't studied world philosophies or early church history, for example, they may not realize that the Christian anthropology expounded by our ancestors still impacts how we walk with the person who is in the process of dying and is asking, "What will happen to me after I die? Where will I go?"

A second reason that I think some seminarians are surprised by how much they are expected to study and to know is that they have been encouraged by some others to see intellectual development and spiritual development as two opposing things. In fact, they sometimes think that academic work undermines our spiritual life. This is simply not true.

It is true that when we study the Bible and the history of interpretation of it, we realize the complexity of how God and God's actions are described. Depending on our previous education, we may be shocked by what we learn, and our image of God may be severely challenged. In turn, our relationship with God can become confusing and turbulent. The process is painful, but in the end, if we choose to remain in relationship, we are closer to understanding what it means to be a person of faith. We are called to be in relationship with a God who cannot be reduced to our simplistic human categories or languages. Having a relationship with God will ultimately require trust and faith, no matter how much we think we know about our Creator.

Still others believe that the Holy Spirit will inspire them to say and to do the right thing at the right time. Consequently, knowing what people have done in ages past is of little importance; what's happening now is what's important. I do not doubt that the Holy Spirit is with us each step of the way in our ministry and in our lives. In fact, I rely on that. Expecting the Holy Spirit to inspire us only in the moment, however, leads to a diminished understanding of the Holy Spirit and the community of believers. If we believe that the Holy Spirit inspired the writing of the Bible, couldn't the Spirit inspire us when we study and write our sermons? I would hope so. And if the Holy Spirit was at work in the lives of our ancestors, wouldn't it be important to listen to what wisdom they learned from the Spirit during their lives? If we didn't study theology or the history of the church, we would miss out on so much of what the Holy Spirit has been teaching us.

YES, THERE IS A LOT TO LEARN

The church is bigger than our experience of it. The world is bigger than our experience of it. And God is bigger than our experience of God. Deep down, we know these things, even if they scare us. They are also why we spend so much time in theological schools on this apprenticeship. The amount of theological material available to us is endless. It can be a challenge, even for faculty, to determine what information and how much of it is necessary for a person to begin in ministry.

Your degree program will likely include a concrete number of required courses and elective courses. Your required courses will be spread out across your time in the program. Required course topics will include New Testament, Old Testament/Hebrew Bible, pastoral theology, educational ministries, worship, preaching, church history, ethics, and theology. In some schools there will be more required topics. In addition to the required courses in each of the subdisciplines of theological studies, the school will likely provide opportunities to take additional elective courses in each field.

However, you'll need to think carefully about how you will use your elective opportunities, because you and your school don't have endless resources. If you have additional denominational requirements, they may dominate your elective options. Depending on the number of credits required by your degree, you may need or want to consider taking more credits than the degree entails. For students in some denominations, it will be necessary to take additional credits beyond what is required for the degree. At some point you'll reach a clear limit of how many courses you can take. You'll have to make choices about what you need to study now and what can wait until later. You'll be required to do continuing education throughout your working life and will have more opportunities to do formal study. Of course, there are financial implications to all these decisions, which you should explore with the student loan officer or other designated person in your school.

In addition to *how many credits* you are taking during any given semester or term, *the number of courses* is also important. For example, three semester credits in a full load of twelve credits could be fulfilled either through one 3-credit course or two 1.5-credit courses. Taking the two 1.5-credit courses is more likely the heavier load, especially if both courses have a major final project.

The balance of courses is also crucial when you are trying to manage the amount of academic work you'll be doing. While schools work hard to ensure a parity of work and reading across courses, there are always some courses that will be more demanding. Taking more than one or two of those demanding courses at once can be debilitating for some students. The key is to come up with a course load for each term or semester that keeps you on track to complete the degree and is manageable for you.

If you pay attention to the rate and amount of material that you'll be studying at any given time, you'll increase the quality and amount of your learning.

IS THERE ONLY ONE WAY TO APPROACH THIS TOPIC?

The demographics within the student bodies of theological schools have been changing significantly. Most classrooms are no longer filled with heterosexual, single, white, Christian males. In the majority of seminaries there are equal numbers of men and women. While white students remain the majority, African American, Latino/a, and Asian students make up approximately one-third of entering MDiv students across ATS schools. In some schools, students will have the opportunity to study alongside people of other faiths, including Judaism, Islam, Buddhism, and Hinduism. In addition to these diversities, the majority of Protestant seminaries advertise themselves as being ecumenical. They take students from numerous denominations and prepare them for ministry in those denominations. Theological schools have anticipated the increased classroom diversity for decades, and we are now seeing and experiencing the benefits and realities of that trend. As classrooms become more diverse in all ways, schools and faculty members are being challenged to consider the parameters of what should be included in the study of Christianity and what sources are considered acceptable for theological reflection.

For example, if human experience[1] is considered a legitimate knowledge resource when reflecting theologically, whose experience is to be included? Does the experience of some get privileged in the definition and the discussion? Within earlier European and American theological discussions, if experience was admitted at all, it was most often limited to that of white men and then labeled as human experience. As the conversation has widened in American theological circles, the experiences of others have been included in the human experience: women, African Americans, Asians, Latinos/as, gays, lesbians, bisexuals, and transgender people. Even with this expansion, greater attention to the diversity of humanity is needed. Furthermore, the relationships that exist among the human family impact how we understand what it means to be human.

How these voices and experiences are added to the conversation remains contested. In some contexts they are added at the end of a conversation or a course, or they are included as optional approaches. The heterosexual, white, male approach to the topic is given place of privilege, and the other voices are considered to the extent that they interact with that dominant narrative. In other programs the diversity of human experience is built into thinking theologically from the beginning. Perspectives that were once dominant are decentered and invited to contribute from their new location as one of the many. In the end, our understanding of the human experience is richer, fuller.

Every school today is being challenged by this increasing diversity within classrooms, churches, and the nation. Each institution is in a different place in the conversation, and most of them will be in an active state of change while you are doing your degree. As a student you have opportunities to give input and to influence the direction of a program or school. For some students this is an important part of their process and of finding their theological voice. Through contributing to the wider institutional conversations, these students are able to clarify where they discern God at work.

There are many other ways to explore and engage the many diversities that are now present in most seminaries. Intense debates with student colleagues, taking theological conflicts into prayer, using course assignments to explore and articulate opposing positions are just a few options. Even if your particular seminary is not that diverse or is diverse in limited ways, you can still make Christian diversity and religious diversity part of your theological education. If you are in a school that won't support the exploration of differing theological positions and perspectives, you'll need to decide how important it is to you. If it is a priority, you may need to find a school that better fits your educational goals.

WORKSHOPS AND CONFERENCES

Every year there are incredible conferences on theological topics across the country. There are also numerous grant-funded programs that are designed to educate seminarians on specific topics or issues. Many of these events explore concerns that won't be sufficiently covered in your degree program. Don't be afraid to ask the program organizers if they have scholarship funding available for seminarians. You can also reduce expenses if you are willing to share travel and room expenses with a colleague. Once you enter into professional ministry, there will be fewer funding sources to support your participation in these programs. Take advantage of every opportunity that you can. The Samuel DeWitt Proctor Conference; the Hispanic Summer Program; the Human Rights Campaign; the Festival of Homiletics; Women's Alliance for Theology, Ethics, and Ritual (WATER); and the Hampton University Ministers' Conference are just a few institutions that offer learning opportunities appropriate for seminarians.

UNDERMINING THE DISTANCE WE PUT
BETWEEN OURSELVES AND OTHERS

Regardless of how diverse or not diverse a theological school is, we will encounter people who think differently from us, either in person or through the assigned class textbooks. Sometimes the most difficult differences to handle are the ones that emerge from a homogenous group. We can easily assume that just because someone has the same skin color, belongs to the same denomination, or has the same sexual orientation, he or she will be theologically similar. There will be numerous opportunities for you to get to know how other people think about God and the life of faith. Many of them will think differently from you. Maybe most of them will. Don't be afraid of them or the differences. Use every opportunity you have to get to know them and their perspectives better. It's not necessary that you agree. What's necessary is to learn how to listen to each other and to learn from each other. In the end you may find you have more in common than you think. This does not mean that we should ignore the harm that some theological perspectives have on people. The challenge is to understand the context and root desire or fear that the person is protecting. Until we understand the other better, we can't enter into a significant conversation about the impact of a particular theological position.

In his book *Between Heaven and Earth: The Religious Worlds People Make and the Scholars Who Study Them*, Robert Orsi makes an important claim that applies to all of us who study religion or theology:

> We may not condone or celebrate the religious practices of others—and let me emphasize this here because it is always misunderstood: to work toward some understanding(s) of troubling religious phenomena is not to endorse or sanction them . . . but we cannot dismiss them as inhuman, so alien to us that they cannot be understood or approached, only contained or obliterated (which is what the language of good/bad religion accomplishes, the obliteration of the other by desire, need, or fear). The point is rather to bring the other into fuller focus within the circumstances of his or her history, relationships, and experiences. It is chastening and liberating to stand in an attitude of disciplined openness and attentiveness before a religious practice or idea or another era or culture on which we do not impose our wishes, dreams, or anxieties.[2]

Orsi is addressing colleagues who study the religious practices and beliefs of others. He makes this plea because he has seen too many theologians and scholars of religion criticize or dismiss the lives of those who practice religion differently from them, without ever making the effort to know the other and their context. The same thing can happen in seminary. Others will appear so different from ourselves that we refuse to see what we hold in common or how we could be them if we had lived the life that they have lived.

Orsi's final comment in this passage helps us to understand how practicing "an attitude of disciplined openness and attentiveness" is also a spiritual practice. When we stand before the other and refrain from projecting our priorities, anxieties, and values onto her or him, we are disciplining ourselves. We make it possible for ourselves and others to take one more step toward each other without doing violence to each other.

INFORMATION IS MORE THAN INFORMATION

Our access to information, thanks to the Internet, is greater than ever before. Search engines and online resources can quickly connect us with data, analysis, and other materials. This reality can desensitize us to the power of ideas and their ability to disturb, confuse, and shape us. There is more to information than data.

The cognitive apprenticeship for professional ministry, therefore, is more than having theological information at your fingertips. In the case of theological education, studying, analyzing, and memorizing are intended to have a formative impact on you. The process is much more than learning information. For example, when you begin studying the history of the Bible, you will learn some specific details about the composition of the biblical canon and the composition of each of the books, which have the power to impact how you conceptualize God's action in the world, think about the Reformation, preach biblical texts, and construct Bible exercises for children and adults. This is just one example. Imagine how many transformative experiences you'll have if you are enrolled in a three-year program!

If you haven't experienced the power of new information yet, you will. Once you do, it's important to pay attention to what it feels like for you to incorporate new ideas into your theological worldview. If you find the information that you are studying troubling, pay attention to that. Allow the questions, mysteries, and dilemmas to surface. Write poetry about them. Sing songs. Paint pictures. Take them to God in prayer. Talk about them with classmates, your spiritual guide, and your faculty adviser. Allow what you are learning to draw you closer to God. It's the questions that will draw you closer, not the conviction of having the right and final answer.

WHAT AM I SUPPOSED TO DO
WITH SOME OF THIS INFORMATION?

There are three particular responses to theological studies that I have seen repeatedly across different schools and students of different denominations. Because they are so common, they deserve special mention.

"This won't preach. I can't use what I am learning in class back in my home church." This will often come up when students are asked to use inclusive language when referring to people and to expand their language for God in their preaching and their assignments. Seminaries don't want students or graduates to take what they have learned and go back into churches and simply repeat what they heard. This would be irresponsible. Instead, we want students to ruminate on what they are learning, to integrate it into their own theological worldview, and to practice different ways of thinking and talking theologically. If students haven't assessed the weight and value of an idea for themselves, they aren't ready to share that information with others. They are also not ready to handle the pastoral needs of those who will struggle with their sharing of unprocessed and undigested theological tidbits. For example, if you are not aware that a prominent figure in Christian history used the metaphor of mother when referring to Jesus, you'll need to spend time with that fact and listen closely to what this powerful and faithful Christian was trying to communicate to the rest of us before you attempt to make the same reference in your ministry.

Your preaching and teaching should always demonstrate that you have studied and thought carefully about what you are presenting. Furthermore, you do not need to share everything you know every time you speak. Knowing when to share particular ideas is just as important as knowing the ideas. As my preaching professor used to say, "We want you to study biblical commentaries as part of your sermon preparation, but when you preach, we do not want to see your exegetical underwear."

"Why haven't I heard about this before? Why hasn't my pastor, who has a master of divinity degree, ever talked about this from the pulpit or in Sunday school?" Someone in a Bible, church history, or theology course inevitably asks this question. It's hard to respond every time it surfaces, because it requires knowing more about the church and the pastor. It's possible that the pastor has talked about the information of concern in the pulpit or in an adult education class, and the student wasn't present to hear it. Maybe the pastor mentioned the item once and didn't feel compelled to repeat it. In some cases pastors don't use their theological education as thoroughly as they could. They don't make it a point to educate their congregation, either in preaching or teaching, about the history of the church or about biblical interpretation.

If you find yourself asking this question, it isn't necessarily a bad thing. It suggests that you comprehend the weight and power of what you are learning. You may experience some frustration and even anger when you learn something about Christianity that reveals that you have been miseducated about your faith tradition. Use that emotional energy to dig deeper into the issue at hand. Research what the consequences were to the particular insight or discovery. Critiquing what you have perceived in your home pastor or church isn't a good use of your time. Instead, spend your time thinking about what you are learning, noticing its impact on you, and asking God in prayer about what God's invitation to you is at this moment of new understanding.

"I am teaching Sunday school next week, and I want to give a lecture on the Old Testament based on what we learned in class last week." I have heard this or similar request nearly every year of my teaching profession. Students will get very excited about what they are learning in class and want to share that information as quickly as possible. Sometimes they will even ask the professor for permission to use the same handouts that were shared by the professor in class. To see students so animated about what they are learning and so willing to include others in their learning is exciting. They sometimes get so enthralled that they start talking about wanting to be a seminary professor, just like their Old Testament professor.

The challenge is that students are not typically ready to begin teaching classes on the Old Testament after attending a course for a few weeks or even a semester. The professor may make teaching look effortless, but it's not. The professor, even in the first year of a career, is bringing numerous years of education and countless hours of study to the topic at hand. They have also given careful consideration to the power connected to what is being taught. They are prepared to deal with the various ways that people may respond to what is being taught.

This response by students is the opposite of the first example above, but the corresponding challenge remains the same. Before either dismissing something as unhelpful to your context or rushing to share it, spend time with the idea or piece of information that is new to you. The more potent the idea is to you, the longer you need to spend time with it. Bring it into conversation with what you thought before taking the class or what you were taught as a child. Consider the ramifications. What are the implications for the church? What are the implications for how we read the Bible? What are the implications for how we relate to God and think about God? What are the implications for *your faith*? Unless you have allowed the teaching to impact your life and faith, you aren't ready to begin professing it to others. You also won't be ready to deal with the emotional responses that some people may have to the material.

One of my favorite illustrations about how important it is for us leaders to wrestle with hard teachings before we begin preaching and teaching is wrestling with Luke 14:25–33, where Jesus turns to the crowds that are following him and lays out the path of discipleship. On his list of admonitions are hating father, mother, wife, children, brothers, and sisters and giving up all one's possessions. This is a hard teaching for us from our brother Jesus. It was hard for the first disciples. Many Christians have spent time with this text. In her book *Leaving Church: A Memoir of Faith*, Barbara Brown Taylor proposes that Jesus was expecting people to find discipleship too difficult and to stop following him. And he wasn't particularly chagrined by that reality either.

When I hear seminarians wrestle with this text, if they take up the challenge, they are often tempted to go in one of two directions. Some are quick to claim, "Jesus didn't really mean that we must hate our mothers and father or give up all our possessions in order to be a disciple. He was simply saying we need to learn detachment." Other students will go the other direction, claiming, "Jesus meant exactly what he said. When you are poor, it is so much easier to rely on God." My response to the students, regardless of which way they lean, is to invite them to wrestle with how they experience the text when they allow it to be written across their own lives. I remind them that they should be cautious about preaching this text if they haven't looked around their own home with this passage in sight. How do they experience this gospel passage when they have a fifty-inch television, a Sleep Number bed, or an Apple watch? Or how do they experience this passage if they have to pick between buying food for their children and putting gas in the car? We have no business preaching or teaching this text if we have not allowed it to speak to our own hearts and lives first.

TESTS AND EXAMINATIONS

Graduate programs tend to require more papers than tests or exams. However, some programs continue to use these practices to assess student learning. Examinations, which tend to cover an entire course or major section of a course, offer students an opportunity to see the larger picture of a course by studying and organizing large amounts of material. Tests require the same, but on a smaller scale. In both cases, preparing for the test or exam requires students to identify, understand, clarify, and organize the major pieces of information addressed in the course. Most graduate programs will emphasize comprehension of ideas over memorization of details. Nonetheless, knowing some details will be essential to understanding the importance of ideas. For example, knowing the year that the printing press was invented (1439 approximately) is crucial to understanding its impact on the Bible, Christianity, and Western culture.

A popular way of talking about tests and exams is to say that they are a way for you and the professor to determine what you know. That may be true. But I have found it more helpful to think about these practices as a way to discover the outer edges of what you know. That is to say, after studying and digesting the material of the course, where are the limits to what you know and understand? What is it that you still don't know about this topic after taking an entire course? Do you still not know what was covered in the course, from numerous angles? This is important to know, because it's the only way you and your professors will be able to identify where you need to focus your intellectual energies as you can continue your education.

READING, RESEARCHING, AND WRITING WELL

A significant amount of your intellectual development and cognitive apprenticeship will be devoted to reading, researching, and writing well.

Depending on your previous educational background, performing these practices within a theological context could be a very new experience for you. Reading a theological book or making a theological argument will have some similarities with reading and arguing in other disciplines, but there will be some major differences. Here are a few things to keep in mind regarding these academic practices.

Reading

Because there will be significant amounts of reading, you'll need to pay attention to what is required reading and what is optional. Not all books need to be read with the same intensity. Develop the ability to skim books that are not required, reading the first and last paragraph or section of each chapter and the first sentence of all paragraphs closely. Take notes on what you read, including the thesis of the book, the intended audience, and a summary of the argument. I have found it helpful to keep these notes inside the back cover of the book. If you are reading electronic texts, store your notes electronically.

Most of the theological texts that you will read will be academic texts, published by academic or denominational presses. They are not devotional texts, though they could easily lead you to deeper devotion. As academic texts they will have a stated position and an argument that is intended to support the position. Many of the books will use a variety of vocabularies, including theological, philosophical, sociological, anthropological, and psychological terms. They will also use a variety of languages, including Greek, Latin, French, German, and Spanish. Get in the habit of having a dictionary within reach when you read. Also, schedule enough time to read some texts twice. Depending on how fast you read, you will likely spend most of your weekly study time reading. This is normal.

When it comes to reading required textbooks, take time to read the opening pages of a book before you begin reading the chapters. Introductions, prefaces, and tables of contents can help prepare you for reading a book and understanding the author's goal and audience. If you don't keep the intended audience in mind as you read the book, you can easily reach false conclusions about the author and the topic.

Don't assume that an assigned book has been included because the professor likes the book or agrees with the argument. Professors assign texts for various reasons. In some cases you need to read a classic text so that you understand the current state of the question, even though the argument in the classic text has been surpassed. Sometimes a professor wants to foment discussion and debate in the classroom, and the textbook was chosen to pressure students into clarifying their ideas and positions. You may not know the reason the reading is assigned until after you have read it.

Your first responsibility is not to decide whether you like the book, author, or argument. You are expected to listen to an author, to understand his or her perspective, to articulate the author's position, and to understand the importance of the author's work. You don't need to agree with it. Once you have demonstrated that you understand the material and the viewpoint of the author, then you can enter into a conversation or debate with him or her. You can also offer a counterargument, as long as you have proven your comprehension of the text at hand.

For those of you who want to do further reading on a particular subject, professors always have more texts that they can suggest. Many professors will share bibliographies of suggested texts.

Some of the books that you will read will lead you into prayer. That's beautiful when it happens. Allow the text to draw you into deeper communion with God. Some assignments will ask you to read a text reflectively. You may want to make some notes about that experience inside the back cover of the book. If you are reading the book for an academic assignment, you'll still need to consider the text from an academic viewpoint. That doesn't mean, however, that your devotional experience with the text has to be kept completely separate from your academic writing. The issue is really about how the two work together. Unless the assignment states this, a faculty member will not be looking for how a text has led you into prayer and will not expect that in a paper. Your spiritual experience with the text, however, can help you to understand the text on a deeper level. It's the deeper understanding of the text that the professor will be seeking. The personal details you can record in your journal.

Researching

Each discipline under the umbrella of theological studies will have a diversity of resources available for your research projects. Your initial challenge is to understand how each of those sources is assessed and used in research projects. In some courses your personal experience will be valuable in assessing how to pull together a series of resources in support of an argument. For example, in a pastoral care course or in a biblical interpretation course, you may have some history with a particular spiritual dilemma or biblical passage. Your experience can't be the measure of the soundness or truthfulness of an argument, but it could help you identify what is missing or unhelpful in a position, theory, or interpretation. Sometimes a professor will ask you to consult academic resources at a particular point in your research process, not earlier or later. When this happens, follow the instructions. The professor has constructed a learning path for the assignment and is likely trying to capture your thinking at critical points. It's also a wise practice to have a clear picture of what ideas or opinions you are taking with you into a research project.

A more recent challenge for students is how to assess online resources. While some reports indicate that online open-source resources have been found to be as accurate as printed encyclopedias of the past, that doesn't mean that they are consistently accurate or acceptable to a professor. The first step in assessing online resources is to consult with your professors in each course. They can guide you on which sources are reliable and which aren't. In some instances a professor will ask you *not* to do any research online but to limit yourself to the texts identified by the professor. Follow the professor's instructions. If a professor does not review the resources available for a given discipline and how to assess the value of those resources, don't hesitate to ask. Your colleagues will need the same guidance. As you increase your knowledge in a particular area, you'll become more capable of evaluating resources for your research and ministry, whether they are online or in print.

Academic integrity is a key value in academic programs but becomes particularly important in theology schools. Cheating on an exam and plagiarism are the two most common violations of academic integrity in theology schools. Failure to act with integrity not only creates a rupture in the trust between faculty and a student but also generates serious concern regarding the moral reasoning of a potential spiritual leader. Lapses in academic integrity will most likely be treated as a violation of the school standards. You should be able to find a school's policy regarding standards violations in the student handbook or manual.

When it comes to researching, a key place where students get themselves into trouble is when they do not take notes properly in the research phase. If you are copying direct language from a source, remember to put quotation marks around the text in your notes and to write down the page number and bibliographical information for the source. Students who do not make it clear in their notes when they are copying down exact text are likely to confuse original composition with a quotation, which can easily lead to a standards violation.

If you have violated the academic integrity standards of your school, you may be tempted to make excuses for your actions or to deny outright the charges. Don't give into those temptations. Instead, be honest and take responsibility for your decisions. If you can be clear about what you did wrong and what you will do differently in the future, you may be able to salvage your place in the program. Making excuses for your actions will only make your situation worse and potentially sabotage what you need to learn from the incident. In some schools and some cases, a single act of plagiarism can result in dismissal from the program.

Some professors or programs will expect you to do group research projects. These can be very challenging but also great learning experiences. With more than one person working on a problem or project you have added wisdom and resources. Learning how to work together is part of the assignment, not an added bonus. Your future work in ministerial settings will require teamwork. Your theology courses are a good place to practice!

Writing

Theological degree programs require a significant amount of writing and different types of it. Research papers, reflection papers, essays, curriculum, worship services, sermons, prayers, pastoral-care verbatims, journal entries, book reviews, and annotated bibliographies are just a few examples! Each of these assignments is a different form that requires a different type of writing you need to cultivate. Learn the differences among these forms. The audience, intention, use of resources, role of your voice, and tone are all different. Parallel examples are a magazine, a newspaper, and a website. In each case there is a variety of written texts with very different forms: articles, announcements, advertisements, sports scores, headlines, editorials, and so on. Each one uses language differently. Those who write in these platforms need to know the differences so that they can communicate effectively. If you intend to communicate effectively, you'll need to know how each format in theological writing works.

There are a lot of misconceptions about good writing. Many people think that the best written text simply flows out of a person without much effort. That is simply not true. Most good writing is the result of multiple drafts and significant editing. If you struggle with writing, you are not alone. You will need to work hard and will need to get help. Some schools will have a writing center; other schools rely on their faculty to provide writing assistance. You also have the option to contract with an outside writing coach. If writing has been a problem for you in the past, get help as soon as possible. Don't wait until your first paper is due.

One of the most effective strategies for increasing the quality of your writing is to focus on the quality of your sentences. Knowing how to craft a good sentence requires knowing what is essential to effective writing, including parts of speech, voice, tone, punctuation, and spelling. Accomplished writers know that good sentences come with significant revision and the removal of all unnecessary words. If you can learn the nuances of individual sentences, you can proceed to paragraphs and entire papers.

Every program will require research papers. In my experience, students struggle the most with these assignments because they don't know how to find appropriate resources and don't know how to utilize the ideas found in those resources. The school library is the best place to begin looking for resources. The librarians are eager to help you find what you need. Your professor can also give you some initial direction about where you can find helpful resources. Once you have identified even a couple of solid resources, you can look at the bibliography listed by those authors to lead you to more resources. If you keep searching in this way, you'll develop a list of resources rather quickly. Your professor will be interested in the variety of resources that you have used and their publication dates. For example, if your bibliography doesn't include anything published in the last few years, your professor may find your research insufficient. Because there is no simple rule that applies to all research papers in all disciplines, it's important to talk with your professor about your bibliography of resources.

After you have familiarized yourself with all your resources, I suggest that you do some writing exercises before you begin writing your paper. Many of the student papers that I read don't get to the heart of the issue until the last page, which is where the paper ideally should have begun. In order to begin writing your paper, you need to know exactly what you are thinking. This can be very difficult to do just by thinking it through in our heads. In order to get clarity about what we are thinking about a topic, we need to get the ideas out onto paper. Here are a couple of options:

— *Writing Exercises.* Set a timer for ten, twenty, or thirty minutes and then write about what you are thinking in relation to the topic. Write as fast you can and with as little stopping as possible. Don't pay attention to grammar or spelling. Most of this writing you won't use in your paper, but the exercise will help you understand more clearly how you are thinking about your topic. You'll also discover pretty quickly if you don't have enough clarity on the topic to begin writing. If your writing exercise results are confused and confusing, it means that you still aren't clear in your mind, and you are not ready to write your paper.

— *Sketching.* Get a large sketch pad or blank sheet of paper, and draw or map your various ideas about the topic. See if you can organize them in a diagram or picture. Play with the different ways that the various authors/voices might work together.

What makes this research paper yours is how you bring together the voices in those texts. You are constructing something that no one has done before. How you do it will partially depend on the details of the course assignment, topic, and argument you wish to make. More than likely, it will take you several attempts to get the balance of voices just right. Many people work best if they create an outline for the paper, after they are clear about what they want to say. This allows you to anticipate problems or gaps in your argument before you begin writing.

There are too many other types of writing to discuss here. At this stage it's important to know that you will be expected to be proficient in a variety of formats and that each professor will explain to you the format expected for a particular assignment. If the professor hasn't written out the expectations, ask her or him to provide them.

WORKING WELL WITH YOUR FACULTY ADVISER

At the beginning of your degree program, you will be linked with a faculty adviser. Most schools will assign you an adviser. Some will give you options. In other cases your adviser is determined by which degree you are seeking. Regardless of the linking process, you'll want to set up an appointment with your adviser as soon as possible. Use the first meeting to help the adviser to know you, your vocational aspirations, and what's important to you about enrolling in the degree program. The success of the relationship depends on both of you. You'll want to do everything you can to help the adviser help you!

When you meet the first time with your adviser, it's a good idea to talk about how your adviser prefers to communicate and to set up appointments. Most professors would prefer not to have an advising session or even set up an appointment while they are getting ready for class or during a class break. Each professor has a preferred method. Some prefer e-mail; others prefer phone calls. Some post sign-up sheets on their office door. Find out what your adviser prefers. Provide her or him with your contact information and how best to reach you.

Below is a list of items that you'll need to address with your adviser. There may be other matters depending on your situation.

Vocational Plans. While some schools will have chaplains and spiritual guides to work with you in the discernment process, your faculty adviser will need to know your thoughts and ideas regarding your vocation if they are going to advise you with course registration and other programmatic decisions.

Course Registration Plan. Most schools require your adviser to approve your course registration plans before you can register. If this is the case, be sure to arrive at your meeting with a plan. Review and know the degree requirements. Don't ask your adviser to tell you what to take. You should also write down any questions you have in advance and bring them with you.

Comprehensive Midprogram Assessment. We described the mid-program assessment process in chapter 2, but it's important to note here that your faculty adviser may play a role in this assessment process. Talk with your adviser about her or his role in the process, and seek her or his input as you prepare for your review session. Your adviser should know you well and be able to help you think about the key issues that you need to address in your self-assessment and review packet.

Denominational Requirements. If your path includes ordained or authorized ministry, your denomination will likely have educational requirements that may or may not be included in your degree program. Sometimes the curriculum of a degree program cannot accommodate the extra courses expected by your denomination. It is your responsibility to know your denominational requirements and to make sure that you are fulfilling them. Share these requirements with your faculty adviser, and together you can strategize about how you will address them during your theological studies. Seminaries are intended to help people prepare for ministry, especially within a denominational context. If you discover you have an ordination requirement that doesn't appear in the curriculum or a particular course doesn't meet your ordination requirement, talk with your adviser about what alternatives are available. These issues can usually be worked out to the satisfaction of the school, the student, and the denomination.

Graduation Requirements. Tracking your fulfillment of graduation requirements is your responsibility. Student handbooks, faculty advisers, and the school registrar are resources for you in this process. In addition, most schools have online student information systems where students can register for courses, view grades, print unofficial transcripts, print tuition invoices, and create degree audits. These audits can help you track which courses and requirements you have completed and which ones remain. Print out a degree audit and take it with you to meetings with your adviser. It will help you remain accountable and make planning easier. There may be some graduation requirements that can't be tracked by the online student information system. It's important to review regularly the requirements that are outlined in the student handbook of the year you entered the program. You may want to bring that to your advising sessions too, especially as you get closer to graduating.

A good relationship with a faculty adviser can make a significant difference in your experience of theological education. In addition to paying attention to the details outlined above, it's good to acknowledge too that there are some roles that are not appropriate for faculty advisers. They are not your parents, friends, pastors, confessors, or therapists.[3] They are professional advisers who are appointed by the institution to assist you with completing your degree and to counsel you on your vocational path.

It's important that there is a bond of trust between the two of you. If the two of you haven't been able to create one, you'll need to address that. Ideally, you will begin by talking directly with the adviser about your concerns. However, if you can't do this, you'll need to talk with the dean of students or another administrator charged with helping students deal with such issues. Their job is to help you deal with the difficulty, not simply to assign you a new adviser. Seminary is not a place where relationship issues can be ignored. They need to be faced. That doesn't mean a new adviser may not be needed at some point; it just means that asking for a new adviser may not address the problem or be in your best educational interest.

ADDITIONAL READING

Barreto, Eric D., ed. *Reading Theologically*. Minneapolis: Fortress Press, 2014.
Goldberg, Natalie. *Writing Down the Bones: Freeing the Writer Within*, 2nd ed. Boston: Shambala, 2005.
Palmer, Parker. *To Know as We Are Known: Education as a Spiritual Journey*. New York: HarperOne, 1993.
Taylor, Barbara Brown. *Leaving Church: A Memoir of Faith*. New York: Harper-Collins, 2006.

5

Cultivating the Practices of Ministry

Marvin was a seminarian in his late twenties and in his second year of preparing to be a pastor of a church. On this particular day it was his turn to play the role of pastor in a workshop organized by the faculty to help students explore particular practices of ministry and to receive feedback. The students took turns practicing as their classmates observed from around the room. A faculty member played the role of a congregant in each scenario.

On this occasion Marvin was going to be practicing a pastoral-care session with Joan, a congregant who had made an appointment to talk with him about her life. He didn't know in advance what issue Joan was bringing to discuss with him.

Joan began the session by confessing that she was a poor mother. Exhausted and distressed, she explained to Pastor Marvin the ways in which she was unable to keep up with all the demands of her children, husband, and home. She shared that her failure as a mother was a sin. She knew that she was failing her family and God. The pastor asked her to name the specific things that she was doing wrong. She dutifully complied, sharing that she was always late with dinner and that she couldn't keep the house clean. Pastor Marvin encouraged her to do better and assured her that she could work harder. He concluded the session by saying that God forgave her, and he sent her on her way. Joan was not consoled and left the appointment still anxious about her spiritual condition.

In the debriefing process Marvin reported that he struggled with how to respond to Joan. He didn't know how to help her and wasn't even sure what he needed to learn in order to provide Joan better pastoral care.

In this brief case Marvin was presented with a common pastoral-care encounter that could occur in any denomination. Joan is struggling because she thinks she isn't fulfilling her obligations as a wife and mother. While she doesn't use the word "discipleship," she clearly makes a connection between her actions and her relationship with God. She comes to the pastor because she needs help moving beyond an interpretation of her life that entails what she experiences as ongoing failure, disappointment, sinful. Marvin simply affirmed her assessment of her life without helping her to question the veracity of her claims. Consequently, he made her condition worse. With more practice at pastoral care, Marvin can learn how to help others examine their life experiences and be cautious when coming to a conclusion about the importance of those experiences. Like Joan, some people need permission to be human, not forgiveness.

Those of us called to the ministry of leading Christian communities are called to help others along the path of discipleship. This means that we are called to serve others, individually and communally, in their relationship with God, without getting in the way. If we want to minister well, we will need to practice. The Holy Spirit provides the gifts (often called charisms) needed to perform the ministry, but we need to develop them.

In this chapter we'll look at the practices of ministry and how they are engaged in the practical apprenticeship of professional theological education.

DISCIPLESHIP AND MINISTRY

In order to understand the practical apprenticeship that is part of professional degrees in theology, it's vital to understand what the practices of ministry are and how they relate to the church and to discipleship. The practice of ministry can't be reduced to a set of techniques or skills. Christian ministry is participation in the life and mission of God through Christ, in a very particular way. It involves putting one's complete self and all one's gifts and talents in the service of the discipleship of others. This offering of oneself requires practice, commitment, and faith.

Among practical theologians there is a discussion about whether all Christian service should be considered ministry.[1] Some propose that the word "ministry" should be reserved for those authorized to lead Christian community and to serve the discipleship of others. Other theologians suggest that using "ministry" for all Christian service is more biblically accurate and secures the idea that the service each one of us provides is important.

What is not up for debate is that all of us have received gifts or talents from God that are meant to be used for the good of all. The use of those gifts is manifested in our discipleship.[2] To be a disciple is to be a person of service. To be even more specific, Christian discipleship or membership in the body of Christ is about putting our gifts at the service of the reign of God. As St. Paul writes in 1 Corinthian 12, each of us is given a different set of gifts that are to be used for the common good. God is at work in each of us; no one should consider himself or herself more important than another. Instead, we all serve one another as members of the same body. Through our discipleship we put our gifts at the service of the whole community. This means that those called to the ministry of leading Christian community must understand their ministry in light of their own discipleship.

In her book *Introducing the Practice of Ministry*, Kathleen Cahalan identifies seven aspects of being a disciple of Christ: follower, worshiper, witness, forgiver, neighbor, prophet, and steward.[3] Cahalan draws this picture of discipleship primarily from the four Gospel accounts and the letters of St. Paul. Cahalan argues that it's important to have a clear understanding of discipleship when thinking about ministry, because these seven aspects of discipleship ground the practices of leading Christian community, which she identifies as ministry.

Cahalan goes on to say that those who have a vocation to ministry receive a particular set of charisms or gifts that are meant to sustain the practices of ministry, which are closely related to the various dimensions of Christian discipleship. She defines ministry as "the leadership of the Christian community through six practices of ministry (teaching, preaching, leading worship and prayer, pastoral care, social ministry, and administration)."[4] Cahalan goes on to say that these practices are grounded in the life of Jesus and in the Spirit-led disciples of the early Christian communities. These six practices of ministry offer us a helpful framework for exploring the practical apprenticeship.

These practices are more complex than they may appear. They require different capacities and demand fluency with different kinds of information. Furthermore, looking at the practices up close would reveal that how those practices are interpreted in the context of ministry will look very different from school to school and from congregation to congregation. The ministerial context and the disciplines associated with it influence how the practice of ministry takes shape in that location. The student, then, is subject to a variety of practices, interpretations, and feedback structures as she or he learns the practices of ministry. Ultimately, the student will need to negotiate those differences as she or he moves toward authorized ministry within a specific context.

Let's take a closer look at each of these practices.

Teaching

Ministers teach in a variety of ways. In fact, much of what ministers do can be summed up as the practice of teaching. The primary focus of a minister's teaching practice is teaching people how to be disciples. Notice that the focus isn't teaching *about* discipleship but about *how* to be a disciple. There is a big difference. Teaching *about* discipleship would allow the teacher and the student to remain at some distance from the challenges and demands that come with being a follower. Learning would be limited to historical, geographical, sociological, and linguistic studies. Instructing others in the path of discipleship does require the wisdom of those disciplines; but it also requires people to teach from within the practice of discipleship. This means that ministers are indeed asked to share a variety of resources through their teaching practice. But they also teach by how they live as disciples, how they show up in the world each day, how they conduct church business, how they preach and lead worship, and how they lead committees.

How does one teach a person how to be a disciple? What does Christian discipleship entail? How does discipleship shape what it means to be human in our current context? What are the acceptable sources for developing a framework for discipleship? What practices or habits does a person need in order to support a life of discipleship? How do or should Christians respond to the reality that Christians don't agree on what constitutes discipleship? What does this mean for the ministry of Christian leadership? These are just a few of the questions that seminarians need to consider as they prepare to engage the practice of teaching as part of their ministry.

From this list of questions you can see that practicing this part of Christian ministry requires a significant amount of information and skill, which are cultivated in the cognitive apprenticeship that we discussed in chapter 4. The seminarian is challenged to research how the insights from studying historical Christian resources can support discipleship in the current age and in each specific context. Insights from biblical texts, biblical commentaries, and early church councils can't be dropped into contemporary Christian life without a significant amount of work, prayer, and wisdom on behalf of a minister.

The language of "teaching," as good teachers know, can be a bit misleading. Good teaching is really about *learning*. It demands paying attention to how people learn. This is especially true in regard to learning how to be a disciple. Effective ministry requires learning about how people learn and then utilizing those insights as one seeks to help others in their path of discipleship. In broad strokes, discipleship is learned through a rhythm of practice and reflection in which people pay attention to how God is calling them along the path. As teachers we provide resources for learning how to listen well. We also lend our eyes and ears to help other disciples remain attentive to the invitations that God is making to them in their path of discipleship.

Master of divinity degree programs will offer at least one course in educational ministry. Many will offer a variety of educational courses. If your seminary offers a lab or practicum on teaching, it would be advisable to take it. Field education or supervised ministry also provides important opportunities to explore the teaching practice of ministry. Use your supervised-ministry assignments as moments to get critical feedback about the extent to which people learn from your teaching.

Some courses in your degree program will include assignments that require you to teach your classmates. These are incredible moments to experiment with new teaching and learning methods. Use these opportunities wisely, seeking concrete feedback from your classmates.

Keeping a journal during your theological studies about your own process of learning would be ideal. Take note about what you have found helpful in your own spiritual development and discipleship path. Identify the resources and practices that have been valuable supports to your practice of faith. Be specific about what was helpful and how those practices or resources worked for you. Pay particular attention to what helped you when discipleship became difficult, dull, unclear, or costly. Being honest with yourself about the challenges of discipleship and what nurtured you in those times will make you a wiser and more compassionate teacher and minister.

Preaching

Preaching is probably the most time consuming of all the practices. Regardless of one's particular ministerial location, ordained ministers are expected to preach. Some preach every day (Roman Catholic priests). Others preach as needed or invited (chaplains). The majority of ordained ministers preach weekly (Protestant ministers).[5]

The reason that preaching requires so much time is because the practice requires interpreting biblical texts, interpreting current disciple experience, composing a presentation, and sharing that presentation with others. In the preaching moment the minister is facilitating an experience with God, the biblical text, and the traditions of Christianity for the gathered disciples. If being a follower of Christ is a key aspect of being a disciple, preaching should help people to understand what that means and how to remain faithful, especially in the moments when following Christ would require that we put ourselves in danger. Healthy doses of humility and transparency are also needed if we intend to keep Christ as the focus of our discipleship.

As a seminarian you will be expected to preach in a variety of settings. You will practice preaching in your preaching classes. If you attend a residential program, you may be required to preach for a seminary chapel service. Most field-education assignments will include preaching. In addition to these programmatic opportunities to hone your skills as a preacher, you will likely have opportunities to be a supply preacher for churches in need. Take every opportunity to preach in different communities and different contexts. Challenge yourself to hear the gospel with Christians who approach discipleship differently from you. Learning to tune your ears to how each community imagines and embodies what it means to be part of the body of Christ will strengthen your skills as an interpreter, listener, and communicator. Faithful preaching is both a spiritual practice and a pastoral one.

One of the challenges for the neophyte preacher is seeking helpful feedback. After spending ten hours preparing to preach, it's understandable to want affirmation regarding the quality of the sermon. The temptation is to settle for comments that make us feel good about what we have done but don't help us to know the impact of what we shared. Soliciting the kind of feedback it takes to learn how to preach more effectively requires some effort on our part. We can't rely solely on the comments we hear in the receiving line at the end of the service. Those comments rarely include how a particular sermon impacted someone's faith or commitment to being a follower of Christ.

If you want to get helpful feedback, you'll need to use sermon-feedback forms or gather a focus group to reflect on your preaching. Most preaching professors will be able to provide you with a sermon-feedback form or help you to create your own. You don't need to ask everyone to fill out a form; you can select a smaller subset, depending on the size of the congregation. You should consider asking someone else to distribute and to collect the feedback forms for you. This allows the congregants some anonymity, which could allow them to share more honestly about the impact of your preaching.

Gathering a focus group of congregants can also be a helpful way to assess the impact of your preaching. You could convene the group yourself, but it could be awkward for both you and the congregants. Instead, ask someone else who is a good group facilitator to recruit participants and to lead the session. Prepare for them a set of questions that you would like them to ask the members of the focus group. Focus your questions on the extent to which the sermon impacted them and on the shape of that impact. The facilitator can then report back to you on the results.

One other important way to develop your skill as a preacher is to review video recordings on your preaching. Seeing ourselves in a video gives us a clear sense of how we are coming across as preachers. Voice intonation, body posture, volume, body movement, and personal appearance can all be easily reviewed with video recording. If your seminary doesn't require you to submit video recordings for your preaching class, you should still record your preaching. Ask your preaching professor or another person whose opinion you respect to review the recording with you and to offer you feedback. Resist the temptation to become defensive. Instead, make yourself available to hear how your performance impacts the listener. Consider the impact that you hope to achieve and imagine how you can adjust your approach to achieve that impact.

Leading Worship and Prayer

Leading others in worship and prayer is a responsibility and a privilege that must be held with care. On the one hand, it requires us to go beyond our own personal spiritual needs. On the other, ministers will struggle to lead others in the worship of God if they aren't aware of the presence and work of the Spirit in their own lives.

As spiritual leaders we are assisting a community of disciples as they seek to live in the presence of God. Consequently, leading worship and prayer is a performance moment. We intend for something to happen during the worship gathering. The majority of congregants get their time with their pastors through weekly worship and prayer services. In some cases this is the only contact a member of the church will have with a pastor. Chaplains lead worship and prayer services too. They are often expected to lead services of different kinds on a regular basis for their institutions. Consequently, the minister's ability to lead worship and prayer is crucial to her or his ministry.

Like preaching, leading worship and prayer requires significant advance preparation. The preparation to lead can begin months, weeks, or days before the service, depending on the context. Worship planning requires knowledge of the particular community of disciples, patterns of Christian prayer, and the dynamics of ritual practice. The moments of leading require performance skills that need to be honed and practiced. They also require being open to the leading of the Spirit. Practicing is important, because there are many issues and dynamics that are hard to anticipate before you have the experience of trying to lead others. Where should you focus your eyes, and how should you hold your hands when you pray? What's the difference between speaking from a pulpit and speaking from the floor where congregants are sitting? How diverse should your language be when you address God in communal prayer? Where should you stand when you are consecrating communion? Should you preach from a manuscript or preach without one? When should the congregation stand? Kneel? Sit down? These are theological and performance matters that must be explored in the classroom and through practice and repetition.

In your Bible, worship, and preaching courses, you'll learn about the various ways that our ancestors worshiped, the postures they used for prayer, and the music they sang. You'll read theological reflections about experiences of worship from both ancestors in the faith and contemporaries. You'll also learn about the diversity of practices across Christian traditions, including the debates over which practices resonate best with Christians today. This body of information is incredibly valuable as you seek to lead Christians today in the worship of God. You don't offer this leadership in a vacuum or outside the history of Christianity. Instead, you join others in the current moment of embodying Christian worship and prayer in the world.

Seminarians have a variety of opportunities to practice the art of leading worship and prayer while in seminary, including, but not limited to, field education, worship courses, home-church worship services, and supply worship leadership at churches in need. Some of you will enter seminary with experience in leading worship and prayer. Some of you will have little or no experience with this part of ministry. Some of you won't have any experience with speaking in public. Regardless, your responsibility isn't limited to gaining experience with speaking in public and leading worship. The charge is to learn how to improve your skills as a worship leader through the practice of leading. You will want to seek feedback from worship participants, but you also need to learn how to pay attention to your own experience of your movement and presence in worship.

As with preaching, making a video recording of your leadership in worship and prayer is extremely valuable. Recordings help us get a sense of how members of a congregation may experience us. They help to focus our attention on any performance issues we may have as worship leaders. Such recordings can help us identify a behavior that may not be an issue in daily life but could become a significant distraction while leading or preaching. When you review the recording, it's good to have at least another person with you, especially a person with whom you have a good trust bond. You need that person to point out behaviors or issues to you, no matter how difficult it may be for you to hear about them. Your vulnerabilities, not your strengths, have much to teach you.

Each seminary will have a particular approach to providing opportunities for you to practice worship leadership. If you need more practice leading worship and prayer than your seminary provides, you can request that the seminary offer more workshops in this area. Another option is to create your own practice sessions with your classmates. Gather a group of six or eight classmates, and take turns performing the various worship roles: proclaiming Scripture, preaching, praying, baptizing, witnessing the exchange of wedding vows, consecrating communion, serving communion, and offering a benediction and dismissal. Record these practice sessions too. When you debrief the

Each seminarian in the communion practicum was required to lead worship and practice consecrating communion. Each one planned the service, created the worship bulletin, and set up the chapel. I instructed the students to wear the appropriate robes for presiding and to treat the practice service as a real worship service. The seminarian's classmates served as the congregation for the practice service. After each practice session, the student and I met to review the video recording.

As I reviewed every video, I would watch carefully to see where the student presiders looked when they prayed. In the majority of cases, the students would look directly into the eyes of the congregants while praying, as if they were speaking to the congregants. When I met with the student to review the video, I would turn the sound off so that we could pay close attention to the student's body posture. At various points I would ask, "To whom are you speaking at this moment in the service?" In many instances, the student would be confused because he or she couldn't tell the difference between addressing the congregation and addressing God. The student's body posture was the same in both instances.

These discrepancies between what the student was saying and how he or she appeared physically allowed us to explore the challenges of addressing God in the midst of an assembly of disciples while making sure that everyone can hear and understand. Underneath the performance challenges was also a theological one: What does our worship communicate about where God is when we gather for worship and prayer?

experience, you may want to go back to a particular moment in the service and examine your performance more closely.

Pastoral Care

On the morning of my first day of ordained ministry I was expected to offer pastoral care to a member of my congregation. I was cleaning up the sanctuary after daily mass when a young woman and her son approached me. I had noticed them at mass because her son was struggling to remain seated during the service, and his mother was struggling to keep him quiet and to remain focused on the liturgy. Although I didn't know it, they were new to the congregation. As soon as the woman introduced herself and her son to me, she began talking about her struggles to care for him and for herself. She was clearly distressed. I remember thinking in the back of my mind, "You should go talk to the priest." Then it hit me. That's exactly what she was doing—and I was the priest! I was ordained, but it took me a long time to live into my vocation.

The practice of offering pastoral care is just as complex as the other practices of ministry. The practice can't be reduced to "helping people." It requires knowledge of the psychological, sociological, physical, financial, and spiritual challenges that people face and how those realities intersect for people in their daily lives. Offering pastoral care also requires a developed ability to listen and to ask questions that help people to understand and to interpret their lives for themselves. Sometimes this requires us to challenge carefully the framework that a person is bringing to their life experience.

The whole practice is further complicated by the fact that, while many people look to the minister to provide God's perspective on their lives, others do not, regardless of the theological tradition of the community. Expectations for what is supposed to happen in pastoral care moments, then, need to be named and negotiated on a regular basis. This requires a practiced humility on the part of the minister. If we want to support people in their ability to make choices and to be responsible for those choices, we can't undermine their agency by constantly telling them what they *should* be doing. However, not every person wants to take responsibility for his or her decisions. Sometimes people seek to shift the responsibility to the minister. Sometimes they are not able to take responsibility for themselves. Their agency is compromised. The unaware and unprepared minister can all too easily become confused about what his or her responsibility is toward those in need of pastoral care.

Each pastoral setting will come with expectations regarding how pastoral care is supposed to be offered. There are significant variations—practical and theological—regarding home visits, hospital visits, communion calls, and office hours. This means that during your theological studies you will need to learn the knowledge and skills necessary for offering pastoral care, and you will also need to learn how to assess and negotiate expectations for pastoral care in various situations.

All MDiv degree programs will require at least one course in pastoral care. They will also offer a variety of electives in the area of pastoral care. You'll also practice pastoral care in your field education or supervised ministry. Clinical pastoral education units provide important opportunities for enhancing one's pastoral-care abilities. Getting feedback on your pastoral-care skills can sometimes be a challenge in a field-education site. If you aren't getting any feedback, you may need to enlist the assistance of your field-education supervisor or the members of your lay committee (if you have one). People may be reluctant to speak with you directly about your pastoral presence but may be more open to share feedback with those who supervise you. Developing a pastoral presence that is healthy, helpful, and faithful takes time and practice. Even if you have extra gifts in this particular aspect of ministry, it's important to develop good habits early in your ministry.

> *Boundary Training.* Most denominations require clergy to participate in boundary training workshops on a regular basis, typically every three years. Most seminaries will require students to participate in some form of boundary training before entering field education or supervised ministry. Some institutions have switched from the language of "boundary training" to the language of "safe space." The shift in language is meant to communicate to communities of faith that safety is more than making sure that pastors or other pastoral leaders keep their hands to themselves. The entire church is responsible for creating a safe space for everyone, especially for those most vulnerable. This includes developing institution-wide policies. It also entails cultivating a community where the agency and worth of every person is respected and supported.

Mercy and Social Justice Ministry

Some people are inspired to enter ministry because they have witnessed the mechanisms and practices of oppression that human beings perpetuate. These disciples already believe that Christ offers a word of judgment against these structures and provides an alternative way of living in the world that supports human flourishing. Theological education provides these disciples with tools, knowledge, and an identity that will support their work of identifying oppressive structures, dismantling them, and setting free those held captive by the powers and principalities in this world.[6]

For others, seminary is the place where they discover the social and political dimensions of Christianity. These seminarians may be inspired to offer care and concern for those in need but have little awareness of the structural dynamics in the world that perpetuate violence, inequity, injustice, and poverty. Becoming aware of the structures of oppression in the world and of our complicity in them is very unsettling. The challenge is to use that discomfort to mobilize oneself and others to constructive action. Theological education provides these disciples concrete paths and practices where they can focus their newfound awareness and energy.

Congregations and their ministerial leaders are well aware of the complexities involved with the practice of offering mercy *and* working for social justice. The challenge is to do both, realizing that there is a tension. Feeding the hungry and clothing the naked are fundamental demands of the gospel. These actions, however, will not bring an end to hunger or poverty. They are necessary acts of mercy for those in need. If we want to minimalize these affronts to human flourishing however, we need to be about dismantling the mechanisms of this world that require hunger and poverty for the benefit of others. Most importantly, we begin this part of our ministerial practice by looking at our own lives and identifying the many ways our ethics and values can be compromised by where and how we use our resources.

One of your responsibilities as a theology student and disciple preparing for ministerial leadership is to understand how your particular denominational and theological context interacts with the gospel demands for offering mercy and working for social justice. Denominations and congregations are not alike or in agreement about what needs to be done or how we should fulfill this part of ministry. If you don't arrive at seminary with an understanding of the various ways that faith communities approach these practices, you'll need to learn them. In addition, you'll need to cultivate your own perspective on these matters in light of discipleship and ministry in your context. No one can do this for you, and there are no shortcuts.

In your academic courses you'll have opportunities to research how our ancestors in the faith handled the demands of mercy and justice. You'll also learn about the ways in which our ancestors failed in these practices of ministry. Through activities in your school, home church, denomination, and field-education site, you'll have plenty of opportunities to offer direct service to those in need. It's important to participate in them. As demanding as they can be, they also foster a sense of satisfaction. Use all those experiences to shape and fuel your work and contribution to dismantling the systems that bring about this oppression of others.

Administration

Whether or not you like dealing with administrative details, the administration of a community is part of the theological practice of an institution. Like Christian worship, the administration of a community of disciples is an aspect of the church's faith in motion. How a community makes decisions, constructs authority, uses power, and handles resources all communicate the values of the group. Denominations use the term "church polity" to describe this dimension of their communal life. Regardless of your comfort with administrative work or your skill level, it's essential to keep the practice as closely connected as possible to the development, support, and leadership of disciples. The more that connection is made concrete for leaders and the community, the more likely it is that everyone will appreciate the administrative dimension of Christianity and Christian community.

Every ministry has an administrative dimension to it, whether it's serving as a senior pastor, youth pastor, or hospital chaplain. Records are expected to be kept. Budgets are needed. Personnel decisions need to be made. Every congregation has an administrative dimension to it, whether or not the community owns its own building or whether the congregation belongs to a denomination or is independent. As soon as God calls a community into existence, administrative matters emerge for the group.

If a congregation is a member of a denomination, some portion of the administrative life of the community may already be determined. Nevertheless, numerous details that are not covered by denominational policy will require the best thinking of the community leaders. New church starts that are not associated with a denomination will have even more decisions to make about the administration of the community. These communities enjoy more options as they are called together. They also have access to the insights and policies of denominational churches, if they wish to consult them. Within the larger arena of Christianity, these emerging communities stand as reminders to all Christian communities about the theological, spiritual, psychological, and social implications of how Christians organize themselves in community. When we take our organizations for granted, we run the risk of perpetuating practices that are ineffective or even contrary to how we understand discipleship.

This is all to say that seminarians need to learn how to practice church administration, including details about finances, buildings, and staff supervision. However, it is perhaps more important that seminarians learn what is at stake theologically in the administrative business of the church. For example, what theological commitment is being embodied when the annual church budget requires the affirmation of the congregation at a congregational meeting? What theological statement is a community making when it decides not to own property but to rent space as needed? There isn't a single, authentically Christian way of organizing the administration of a community of disciples called together by God. There are many ways to do so. Some have existed for centuries. Other ways are emerging as Christianity encounters the benefits and the brokenness of human existence in the twenty-first century.

Consequently, the practice of administration is an act of leadership. The minister assists the community in making its theological commitments manifest in the ways that it organizes its life together. The seminarian who hopes to lead a community of disciples in the future would do well to study closely what is at stake in the variety of ways in which Christians have organized and are organizing themselves. Furthermore, the healthy leader is able to distinguish what's in the best interest of the community, regardless of what is appealing or beneficial to the leader.[7] There is an element of selflessness, then, at the heart of leadership that seminarians and pastors need to cultivate. This doesn't mean that the minister's needs are unimportant or that it's permissible for ministry to be damaging to the minister's selfhood. It means that the well-being and mission of the entire community comes before the desires or preferences of the leader. For example, the pastor's desire for a raise in order to go on a dream vacation cannot be the driving force behind a church's stewardship campaign. A decision regarding the relocation of a congregation cannot be dictated by where the pastor would like to live.

Unless you are pastoring a church while doing your theological studies, it can be difficult to get experience with the practice of administration while in seminary. Seminarians are typically not entrusted with leadership positions in their field-education sites. Instead, they are invited to observe the practice of administration in a community.

A seminarian can learn a lot by carefully observing the administrative practices of a community and a supervisor. Having a supervisor who is willing to talk with you about how and why decisions are made in the community is essential to learning what's at stake in this practice of ministry. Seek out field-education sites where supervisors and members are willing to talk openly about this dimension of ministry. Because you will bring a new set of eyes and ears to the conversation, your questions may stimulate more reflection about the practice of administration and its pastoral and theological implications.

Most, if not all, seminaries offer a course in church or institutional administration. Schools will also offer a variety of courses covering the various ways that denominations govern themselves and handle church administration. These are labeled polity courses, and you'll be expected to take one of them if you intend to minister within a denominational context.[8] These courses are designed to help seminarians learn what it will mean to provide leadership within a particular denomination and to understand the connection between the organization of the community and its theological views.

Many seminaries will offer additional workshops to address specific dimensions of the practice of administration. Denominations will often offer workshops and special training sessions on stewardship, church finances, the cultivation of church trustees or board members, and other topics related to the practice of administration. Whether or not the course on administration is required for your degree, take it.[9]

Congregations can develop serious financial and legal problems if the leadership does not understand and follow regulations regarding institutional finances. An illustration that's not difficult to imagine is church leadership repeatedly using restricted endowment funds to cover shortfalls in other areas of the annual budget. As these actions become public, the integrity of the church and its leadership is compromised. Church giving declines because members are unsure of how money is being handled, despite how well things may seem in other aspects of the life of the church. If the leadership does not address the problem directly, honestly, and immediately, the entire life of the community is put in jeopardy. This is the kind of problem that can be avoided when the leadership and ethical dimensions of church administration are understood.

If you are seeking ordination in a denomination, those who approve candidates for ordination will expect this to be on your transcript.

FIELD EDUCATION/SUPERVISED MINISTRY

Field education is a key requirement in the master of divinity degree program, because it serves as a bridge between the other aspects of the degree and the student's ministerial practice. Advisers, supervisors, faculty members, and denominational leaders are able to witness how a seminarian performs ministerially. When a seminarian preaches or teaches in the field-education site, she or he has an opportunity to develop discernment skills, interpretation skills, and communication skills. Consequently, those involved in observing the ministry of the seminarian can assist in helping the student to reflect theologically on what is happening in the student's practice and what that means for the student's vocational discernment. Because most students will do part of their field-education requirement in one of their denomination's churches, they will also get firsthand experience with practicing theological reflection in a particular denominational context and a particular congregational context.

Integrating Field Education and Coursework

One of the biggest challenges for seminarians in their field-education or supervised-ministry sites is learning how to integrate what they are learning in the seminary classroom and what they are learning at the field site. The charge isn't for seminarians to gather up information in their seminary classes and then deliver that information to the people in a congregation. Seminarians—and pastors, for that matter—are not charged with information delivery. Most of the resources that seminarians will work with in their courses do not provide packaged data that a seminarian can use immediately or store for future use. Seminary introduces students to resources that they can use in pastoral ministry. However, those resources—for example, the Bible, documents from church history, and theological treatises—require knowledge, skills, and capacities to be able to use them for the benefit of discipleship.

Practicing how to use the resources from our extensive Christian heritage will take place in seminary classrooms and in field-education sites. The classroom provides students with chances to experiment and take risks without endangering the spiritual well-being of a congregation. Seminarians need these opportunities to sharpen their skills and to see what's possible in their preaching and teaching. Field-education sites provide seminarians with opportunities to serve a community in their process of growing in their discipleship. The stakes are higher than they are in the classroom, because these practice moments involve an actual community of disciples and their spiritual welfare. Risks can be taken, but seminarians need to calculate those risks, with the help of their lay and ordained supervisors in the field.

Fundamental to what a seminarian offers a field-education site is a person who is learning how to discern the presence and call of God to a community in a particular time and place. Like the pastor, the seminarian isn't expected to provide the answers to the discernment questions of a community of disciples. Rather, the seminarian joins the community along the path of discipleship, open to exchanging stories about God's presence and action in the world and what that means for Christian disciples.

Building Capacities One Step at a Time

Students enter into field education with a variety of backgrounds and skills. No two seminarians are exactly alike. Each field site too has particular needs and dynamics. As you consider possible sites and supervisors, you will need to join the community in discerning what the best fit is for all parties involved. During that process you'll begin to imagine what your learning covenant would look like if you decided to do field education in that place. If a field placement and supervisor aren't able to offer you opportunities to explore and learn the practices of ministry that are important to your formation as a minister, you'll need to find a more suitable location. The fit must be good for the student, the supervisor, and the site.

Students are often eager to begin engaging the practices of ministry, but they don't always have experience or understand the prerequisite skills needed for those practices. For example, the student who has no experience with teaching and hasn't taken the required seminary course on educational ministries should consider serving as a teaching assistant to a more experienced teacher before taking on the role of lead teacher. Even as an assistant the seminarian can participate in developing lesson plans, lead discussions, and offer short didactic sessions. Eventually the seminarian can be the lead teacher, and the supervisor can observe the student's work and offer feedback. Or students who have little or no experience with reading or speaking in public shouldn't jump directly into preaching. Instead, writing prayers, proclaiming Scripture, and offering the pastoral prayer at worship services are better places to begin.

In the latter part of one's field education, it is important to get experience with the more complex dimensions of ministry. Learning how to plan and lead worship is critical and requires numerous intellectual and practical skills. Preaching requires the same. Preparing agendas for meetings and leading people in committee meetings and tasks are other skills that require multiple organizational and social skills. Engaging conflict on a community level is another complex aspect of ministry that requires good listening skills, the ability to be a nonanxious presence, and knowledge regarding the dynamics of communal conflict.

The challenge is for the seminarian, the supervisor, and the seminarian's adviser to work together to establish the kind of learning the student needs at the particular point of her or his formation. The educational needs of the seminarian, not the needs of the supervisor or site, must come first. This is why field education supervisors need to be experienced and mature practitioners. It can be too easy for the needs of the supervisor or field site to dictate the learning agreement with the student. Each field education site has real needs that must be addressed, and it is very easy to rely on a seminarian to fix the problem. In the ideal world the supervisor or faculty adviser will make sure that the educational needs of the student are protected. However, the seminarian must also remain alert and attentive to the skills and capacities that she or he needs to develop.

Giving and Receiving Feedback

By the time students arrive at a graduate program, they are very familiar with giving and receiving feedback in a classroom setting. However, many do not have experience with giving and receiving feedback in a collegial working context. Field-education supervisors and lay committees at a field site will be asked to complete feedback forms regarding the ministry performance of the seminarian. Those comments are supposed to be reviewed and discussed with the student in person. In addition, the seminarian will be expected to provide feedback regarding the supervisor and the site, which are also supposed to be discussed in person.

Because there is an imbalance of power, seminarians need to be clear about what is being asked of them. These moments are not about whether a seminarian liked or didn't like the site or supervisor. The feedback process is intended to help the supervisor understand how actions taken at the field site impacted the seminarian. Just like the seminarian, the accomplished supervisor wants to learn how to achieve her or his intended results. Feedback is an important part of that process. Seminarians would be wise to consider that the supervisor could be their colleague for many years to come. Building a healthy, authentic, collegial, and constructive relationship with colleagues while in seminary will bring many benefits in the years ahead.

ADDITIONAL READING

Barton, Ruth Haley. *Strengthening the Soul of Your Leadership: Seeking God in the Crucible of Ministry.* Downers Grove, IL: InterVarsity, 2008.
Friedman, Edwin H. *A Failure of Nerve: Leadership in the Age of the Quick Fix.* New York: Church Publishing, 2007.

6

Shaping an Identity for Ministry

Many years ago I worked in a seminary program with a student named Clark. During one of his review sessions, he offered me his understanding of the formation program of the seminary. He said, "It feels like taking off a costume, a bunny costume that I've been wearing a long time and didn't even know it. As I take off portions of the costume, I am coming to know and understand myself in ways that I never imagined. It's a little scary at times, but it is also very exciting. I thought that I knew myself, but all along I was looking at the bunny costume and not myself."

Clark came to the seminary after several years in military service. He had his hair cut so often that I never saw it change. His clothing was precise, and his shoes always polished. There wasn't a friendlier seminarian in the school; yet he was cautious and stiff. I found him hard to know. Maybe it was because I was his superior in the seminary system, which has a lot of similarities to the military. He was used to approaching his military superiors with caution, respect, and deference. He simply approached me in the same way, but I am not completely sure that he understood that. Clark was so obedient and earnest that it was often hard to tell what was really happening with him on the inside. I often thought that instead of telling me the truth about what he was thinking and feeling, he said what he had perceived to be the appropriate way to think and feel.

It wasn't until we sat down for that review session that I realized that one of Clark's central challenges was that he didn't really know what he thought and felt about what he was learning and doing in his theology program. This was the first time in his life that he was expected to share his personal perspective. In fact, it was the first time in his adult life that he was allowed to have a personal opinion. He came to seminary in order to become a priest. His first assignment was to find out who he was.

While I have never heard another seminarian talk about their experience of a seminary formation program in quite the same way that Clark did, I have heard many students describe the journey in very similar ways. Over the years, I have witnessed a tremendous amount of discovery, growth, and transformation in students.[1]

I wasn't all that different from Clark when I was a seminarian. I was obedient and sincere too, not because I came from military service, but because I was very naive. I had no idea of who I was or how I felt about almost anything. Early in my first year of theological studies I was required to create a list of personal goals. Thanks to the wisdom of my faculty adviser, I decided that I would focus some of my attention on my emotional development. My director suggested that I focus specifically on the emotion of anger. I thought that I had very little experience with it; I thought of myself as a happy person but agreed to the suggestion. During that year I read books about anger, listened to audio presentations, went to workshops, and talked a lot about it with my faculty adviser, spiritual director, and seminary colleagues. To my surprise, I realized that I got angry a lot; I just didn't have the permission to acknowledge it or the language to interpret it.

I remained in seminary formation for another four years and continued to focus my attention on my emotional life. I attended an American seminary in Belgium. Living so far away from home for so many years meant that I had a steady stream of emotional experiences, some of them very intense: love, betrayal, exhilaration, failure, joy, despair, and anxiety. There was no way that I could avoid them if I wanted to function healthily, let alone grow spiritually, emotionally, and ministerially.

It would be easy to think that the location and context of my theological studies in such an unusual place made my experience somewhat unique. I don't think that is true. In fact, while working in American seminaries for the last twenty years, I have seen many seminarians work through the same set of issues that Clark and I did. One place where my experience differed from Clark's was that he had more time to discover that he was wearing a costume when he arrived at seminary and more time to figure out how to take it off. His experience didn't have quite the same urgency that mine did. Mine was much more abrupt. The radical separation from my support system at home left me vulnerable and emotionally fragile. I needed to find help from the very beginning so that I could function and begin to connect what I was feeling with what I was learning in my theology classes and at my field-education placement.

Becoming a spiritual leader is not a smooth and effortless process. It's more like running several marathons back-to-back and realizing that you won't be able to finish without extreme effort and a lot of support. It's about being pushed to our limits and seeing what we do when we get there. The time spent in seminary is only a portion of your spiritual development, but it's an important part. There is a lot of training done within a short period of time with the expectation that significant growth will take place.

IDENTITY, INSECURITIES, AND FALSE IDENTITIES

Who am I? What is my identity? What is underneath the costume or behind the mask that I wear each day? These are a few of the fundamental questions involved in the identify-formation apprenticeship that each student is expected to answer. Within the process, students are repeatedly asked to reflect on their experience, including their experience of themselves. They are asked to interrogate, examine, and describe the various ways that they, along with others, work to shore up identities or false selves that distract us from seeing ourselves as God sees us.

Human beings have been asking these questions for thousands of years, and each religious tradition has various ways of exploring those questions. The questions are not as easy to answer as we may think. Like Clark, we may find out that what we thought was our identity is simply a costume that we have been wearing for a long time. Or we may be tempted to take a shortcut in dealing with these questions, looking to copy or adopt the answers of someone else. But there are no shortcuts. We have to struggle with the questions ourselves. No one can walk the path of faith for us. Without knowing who we are, our spiritual growth will be minimal, and our ability to lead will be compromised.

Before Jesus entered into his public ministry, he needed his identity to be made clear too. All four Gospels stress Jesus' identity in their

opening chapters. John declares that Jesus is the light of the world, the
Word became flesh, God the only Son, and the Lamb of God. Matthew,
Mark, and Luke disclose Jesus' identity when he is baptized by John. As
Matthew tells the story, John baptizes Jesus in the Jordan River, despite
John's protest that it should be the other way around. The Common
English Bible interprets what comes next this way: "So John agreed to
baptize Jesus. When Jesus was baptized, he immediately came up out
of the water. Heaven was opened to him, and he saw the Spirt of God
coming down like a dove and resting on him. A voice from heaven said,
'This is my Son whom I dearly love; I find happiness in him'" (Matt.
3:15b–17). Even if Jesus already had a sense of God's love for him, this
must have been a life-changing moment. God declared Jesus' identity
and announced that God finds happiness in him.

When we reflect on the life of Jesus, it makes perfect sense that
knowing his identity before he entered into his public life and ministry
was crucial if he was going to face the temptations, distractions,
belittlement, betrayal, and execution that ensued. The same is true for
us. Our lives may not include complete betrayal and execution, but
they will certainly include temptations, distractions, and belittlement.

In my years of serving in ministry, I have had my share of distractions
and temptations. There is always someplace else where I think that life
would be easier or my gifts would be more appreciated or I could be
more successful. I've also had my share of belittlement, including some
nasty mail from people who wished to discredit my commitment to the
gospel and the church. But most of the temptations and belittlement
have come from within me. When things go well, it's only too easy to
think that I am responsible for all the good things happening in my
life. And when things get difficult, it's easy to despair that I am not
prepared or capable to meet the challenges that I face. In either case
I can be quick to draw up the mental list of evidence to support my
claim of being awesome or being worthless! Both paths of thought lead
me away from my identity as a beloved child of God and frustrate my
ability to hear the Spirt of God speaking to me.

Jesus warns us that there are many other distractions that can get in
the way of our knowing our identities. We can be tempted to confuse
the human labels—sibling, child, elder, parent, citizen, alien, righteous,
faithful, unclean, outcast—with our true identities as beloved of God.
If we intend to claim our identities in God, we'll need to let go of all
the other ways that we create false ones.

In Greek, the word *krisis* ("crisis") is first translated as "a separating, a sundering," or "separation."[2] In other words, a time of crisis is a moment when we sift and separate one thing from another. We judge between what is most important to us and what is not. Becoming a disciple of Jesus, then, is a moment of crisis. It's a moment when we are pushed to respond to God's declaration of our identity. Embracing our identity in God might be easier if we didn't have to leave all the other identities behind. In addition to those other identities, we may also have to leave behind some ideas, assumptions, and perspectives about God, Jesus, the Holy Spirit, the Bible, the church, and humanity that we held dear.

Seminary is another moment of crisis because it demands that we renew and deepen our commitment to our true identity and experience the consequences of embracing that identity. There is no way that we will be able to help others in their discipleship if we aren't fully engaged with our own. To put it another way, going to seminary is a lot like entering the wilderness.

SEMINARY: ENTERING THE WILDERNESS

When people share with their family, friends, and church family that they are going to seminary, there is bound to be someone who will offer this admonition: "Don't lose your faith at the seminary. Don't let them take it away from you." When seminarians share that with me, it's always a bit hard to know how to respond. The truth is that seminary does affect our faith. It's intended to do that. Our faith is supposed to grow and to be transformed through the process. If at graduation our faith is the same as it was when we entered, the educational experience will have served no purpose.

Think of a red oak tree. In the summer, the leaves are shiny green and fill out every branch. As fall arrives, the leaves turn brilliant shades of red. As winter approaches, they turn brown. Eventually the tree will let them go as new leaves emerge. Our lives are like that of the oak. Year to year there are parts of us that grow but remain relatively the same (limbs, bark, and roots), but there are also other parts of us that we release, even though they were essential to us for a time (leaves). There is no way that we can grow without letting go of some of the ideas, practices, and perspectives that served us, well or not so well, in our earlier life.

In the Gospel according to Matthew, Jesus told his disciples early in his ministry, "Where your treasure is, there your heart will be also" (Matt. 6:21). Jesus could make this kind of statement because he took himself to the wilderness *so that* he would be tempted. He knew that there was no way he could be sure of what was most important unless he was put to the test. Not only did he go to the desert; he also fasted for forty days. In other words, he pushed himself to the outer limits of his humanity, knowing that how he behaved at that moment would tell him the truth about what he treasured.

Entering seminary is a lot like entering the wilderness. We take leave of the people with whom we regularly surround ourselves and go off on a journey. Even if we are doing a completely online program, there is still some sense that we are entering into a process on our own. Our family and friends may support us, but they can't do any of the work for us. In this wilderness we are confronted with challenges to our knowledge, beliefs, identities, and skills. Some of us will be tempted to rely on our intellectual abilities; others, on pastoral skills or personal charms; still others, on previous privileges. But all these treasures will not save us when we are struggling with the deepest challenges of living out the gospel and embracing the challenge of spiritual leadership. Eventually we will need to embrace our identities in God, if we hope to have the strength to grow in seminary and in ministry.

SPIRITUAL PRACTICES

Most of us enter seminary with a very diminished or narrow understanding of spirituality or spiritual practices. We can too facilely limit the use of the label "spiritual practice" to prayer moments, devotions, worship, and Bible study. However, study, time with friends and family, rest, and pastoral work are also part of our spiritual lives. The truth is that everything is part of our spiritual lives.

A seminary will expect you to arrive at your theological studies with some experience with prayer and the ability to share your understanding of God with others. No one will expect you to be a mystic or fully enlightened. Each person will bring with him or her a set of spiritual practices. During the course of your program, you will likely be required to expand your set of spiritual practices and to experiment with a variety of spiritual practices from different traditions within Christianity. Beyond trying the different practices, you'll be asked to share with others how those practices affected you and your relationships, including your relationship with God.

Your studies and your intellectual development will have a particularly strong impact on your spiritual development. For many students this comes as a surprise, because they didn't realize that how much our thoughts *about* God influence our prayer and our relationship with God. As students learn more about the various ways that God has been understood throughout history, their own image of God is closely analyzed and often challenged.

Furthermore, when students realize that there is gap between who God is in God's self and the various ways in which God has been described or experienced throughout history, they can respond in a number of ways. Some become very confused; some grieve the loss of the certainty that their previous God language provided; still others find this gap to be tremendously freeing. Whatever his or her response, everyone experiences some level of theological disequilibrium. This is perfectly normal and expected.

What doesn't get said often enough in seminaries is that we need to take all our experiences—including our responses to what we are learning about God and Christianity in history—into our time of prayer. There isn't anything that we can't take to God for conversation and reflection. If a large part of our ministry includes talking *to God* and talking *about God* to others, we must develop a comfort with the diversity and the ambiguity that comes with God language.

Writing as a Spiritual Practice

Writing can be a powerful spiritual practice for people, especially during theological studies. In the course of one day, a person can have so many experiences that there isn't time to process them. This used to happen to me all the time when I was in seminary. Sometimes the dinner conversation at the seminary was so intense that I needed to go back to my room to reflect on what I was thinking and feeling about what was said. Writing in my journal was one of the best places for me to explore what happened; what I was feeling about what happened; and what, if anything, I needed to do in response. Most of the time I didn't need to respond, but I did need to write out the experience so that I could understand what had happened.

Over the years I have found two types of writing practices to be helpful in my spiritual life. The first type is called daily pages. Julia Cameron created this structure for herself and has written about it in *The Artist's Way*.[3] The practice is deceptively simple. The first thing every morning you handwrite three pages in your journal, no matter how long it takes. Once you begin, you are to keep writing without lifting the pen from the paper. You can write about anything that you like, and you don't need to worry about grammar or punctuation. If you get stuck, it's helpful to have a phrase or saying to keep you going. I tell my students to begin writing the nursery rhyme "Mary Had a Little Lamb" if they find themselves at a loss for words. Most people have no difficulty writing the three pages each day. Cameron recommends not reading over what we have written right away. Instead, it's best to wait until we have been writing for a month or two before we look back over what we have written. The point isn't so much to observe what we said on a particular day but to look for trends in our writing over the course of time. What do we write about? What does it say about us? What does it say about what's on our mind?

The second type of writing practice comes from Natalie Goldberg.[4] Goldberg promotes timed writing exercises. The writing period could be ten minutes or more. It's probably good to begin with shorter periods and work up to longer ones. Each time period begins with a prompt, which we put at the top of a page. We set a timer for the session and then begin writing. As in Cameron's version, we are not to stop, keeping the pen to paper, until the timer rings. I will often do four or five timed writing periods in one sitting. You can use any prompt you like, but it is helpful to keep a running list somewhere in your writing notebook. One way to generate some interesting writing prompts is to do a couple of timed writing sessions with the prompt "I remember . . ." Our minds can release all sorts of things during these writing sessions. As we look over the list of things we remember, we will be able to spot the topics that are worth more exploration. Simply put that prompt at the top of a page, set the timer, and write!

If you do use either of these writing exercise for thirty days, I guarantee that you'll learn something about yourself. You'll learn what's important to you, because it will keep surfacing in your writings. If you are obsessed with some idea, person, or thing, it will emerge in your writing. When you look back over your writings over a longer period, you'll find out where your mind spends its time when you are trying to focus on other things. As we all can testify, our minds are not always where our bodies are. This is why this type of writing is considered a spiritual practice. It helps us to be present in the moment. We humans are easily distracted and all too often absent from the present moment. We are thinking about what happened yesterday, what we will eat for dinner tonight, or what we think could happen tomorrow. Or we are passively pondering our most recent obsession. When we allow our attention to be diverted in this way, we miss the ways in which God and others are speaking to us in the present. Writing is a powerful tool and practice that can bring clarity to our relationship with God, others, and ourselves.

Worship

Christianity is a communal religion. As St. Paul says in 1 Corinthians 12:12–13, "For just as the body is one and has many members, and all the members of the body, though many, are one body, so it is with Christ. For in the one Spirit we were all baptized into one body—Jews or Greeks, slaves or free—and we were all made to drink of one Spirit." In our worship, we gather as a body to give praise to God and to practice being the body of Christ so that we can live more fully as that body at every moment. Participation in regular Christian worship takes on additional importance as you undertake your theological studies. You will be asked to participate regularly in community worship and to provide some worship leadership at the seminary and in your home church. If you are in an online program, you won't be expected at campus worship, but you will still be expected to participate in a worship community.

As you take on leadership roles within worship, you will need to learn how to pray and to lead at the same time. This will take time. For some it doesn't come until after several years of ministry. In my first year of ordained ministry, I was too nervous to pray while leading the service. I was focused on what I and the other ministers were supposed to be doing. Over time, as I got more comfortable and confident in my role, I was able to join the community in prayer.

Most seminaries will expect students in residential programs to participate in worship at the seminary, even if you belong to a congregation or are the pastor of the congregation. Worship is an important part of community life in a seminary. It's the place where the entire community brings its thoughts and words about God into its relationship with God.

It's also important for theology students to participate in worship services where you aren't in leadership, even if you are already pastoring a church. We all have moments of stress, confusion, and doubt. In those moments, it's necessary to have worship opportunities where we are not in leadership. In fact, there will likely be moments during your studies when you will lose your theological voice or fumble for authentic words to speak to God or to speak about God. It's a natural response to being exposed to so many different and competing theological viewpoints. When those moments arise, it's paramount to be able to attend worship services that are not dependent on you. Even if we find ourselves without words or incapable of fully participating, we can be carried along in the prayer of the community. It's a humbling experience, but a valuable one for anyone who intends to lead a community in prayer.

Spiritual Guidance/Direction

Externally there is a lot happening with students in theological studies. In addition to many hours of studying, writing, and dialoguing with colleagues, there are hours spent in a field placement where people are supervising your participation and leadership. Within the course of a semester, students will have been exposed to a variety of ideas, challenged to expand what they know of Christian faith, and given direct feedback on their pastoral practice. This is a lot of information to process, emotionally and spiritually. As we discussed in chapter 4, a faculty adviser is a valuable resource for helping students to digest and process what they are experiencing. However, the conversations with a faculty adviser are not privileged ones. Faculty advisers are responsible for helping the entire faculty assess the progress of a student in the program and readiness for ministry. Because these conversations are not private, a student needs to treat them as professional coaching sessions. They are not intended to be therapeutic or confidential, no matter how helpful they are to the student.

Spiritual direction or spiritual guidance, on the other hand, is confidential. The information that a person shares in those conversations is completely private. Even if a seminary requires a student to work with a spiritual director, the content of the sessions remains confidential. All the director can share with the seminary is to confirm that the student is working with the director.

The issue of privacy in this relationship is important, because it provides students with space to talk about how the entire seminary process is affecting the student's relationship with God. This includes talking about how the student prays and exploring what happens in those moments of prayer. The director provides another set of ears and eyes to help a directee pay attention for God's activity in her or his life.

Having attended a Roman Catholic seminary, I was required to have a spiritual director at all times. Consequently, I can't imagine attending seminary without having a director. I have been in spiritual direction for more than thirty-five years. While I was in seminary, I met with my director every two weeks. It was the safest place for me to talk about my changing sense of self as I studied the Bible and other theological texts. All my relationships were evolving at the same time as well. My time with God was one of the only constants that I had in my life and one of the few places where I could bring all my thoughts, desires, and brokenness. I needed a spiritual guide to help me listen for what God was trying to tell me, for what God was asking me to do, and for how God wanted to be with me. There were some moments when I thought nothing was happening when I prayed. At other times my life felt too busy to pray. My director kept bringing me back to my relationship with God and helped to steady my listening.

If you aren't familiar with spiritual guidance or spiritual direction, you can find helpful information and resources on the website of Spiritual Directors International, www.sdiworld.org. There is a tool on the website that can help you locate a director in your area. If you decide to pursue this spiritual practice, I recommend that you interview three or four potential directors before deciding which one would be a good fit for you. There are different approaches to spiritual guidance, and one may work better than others for you.

Daily Prayer

A commitment to daily prayer, or at least regular prayer, may seem like an obvious practice for a minister and for a seminarian, but in my experience it's not. Taking time for prayer on a regular basis is a real challenge for everyone, including pastors. When I have taught spiritual formation classes and required students to commit to praying two times each day for three weeks, some students would remark afterward that the practice helped them to see that they had had an inaccurate picture of their prayer life. They had resisted being forced into praying at specific times, arguing that they prayed all the time, as St. Paul commended in 1 Thessalonians 5:17. But during the practice period they realized that they had been fooling themselves. The intentional prayer times enriched their prayer and their relationship with God.

One of the expectations for most Christian ministers is that the minister be a person of prayer. This isn't limited to the minister knowing how to pray, publicly and privately. The minister is expected to be a person who prays—for themselves and for the many needs of all. They are called to bring to God on a regular basis the needs of congregants, the local church community, the nation, and the world. This charge is both a pastoral one and a theological one. It's pastoral in the sense that a minister is called to care for the spiritual needs of a community. Praying for the members of that community is part of that responsibility. It's theological in the sense that the minister leads a community as it intercedes with God on behalf of the entire world. This is not to say that all Christians aren't called to the same life of prayer. They are. The ordained minister, however, leads the community in this charge.

Seminarians should begin taking up this charge during their time in seminary, praying for the needs of others on a daily basis. To help with this practice, it would be wise to look for resources that gather petitions for the benefit of the church and world. The ancient practice of the daily hours or the daily office is one place where seminarians can find such petitions. There are numerous versions available, including online ones. Some denominations will also publish petitions for all clergy and congregations to include in their prayers.

Holding the desires, fears, thanksgivings, and despairs of others before God is a humbling experience and a significant part of the identity-formation apprenticeship. Praying for others changes us. Each time, day after day, we turn ourselves toward God and lay bare the realities of life on earth. In the process we are invited to decenter ourselves for the benefit of all. The intention is not to silence or disregard our own needs but to enlarge the boundaries of what we hold before God. When it's too easy to forget those who hunger for food, those who are wounded by war, or those who are dying alone, the prayers of the church expand our narrow vision. Holding the needs of the entire world will also affect the way we preach, teach, and lead. It unites us with the fullness of the body of Christ and helps us to discern the direction and focus of the church's work.

Self-Examination, Confession, and Reconciliation

It is essential that we as Christians acknowledge our capacity for sin and our need for reconciliation. Our growth in Christ requires us to be honest with ourselves and with God about our need for forgiveness. As spiritual leaders it becomes even more important for us to admit when we have committed an offense. We don't necessarily need to make our confessions public, but it is important for people to know that we are willing to admit when we have been wrong and to make restitution.

There is one thing that you can know for sure about your time as a member of a seminary community—any community actually. Someone will disappoint you, and you will disappoint others. It's simply inevitable. We will fail one another if not outright hurt one another. This is the human condition.

What always remains to be seen is what we will do when we hurt each other. Will we acknowledge what we have done? Will we apologize? Will we work not to do it again? Will we ask for forgiveness? Will we speak up when we have been offended? Will we receive the request for forgiveness? How will we respond? Will we allow ourselves to be softened, not hardened, by the experience, whether we are the one who made the offense or the one who has been offended?

When someone offends us or when we are the one who has offended someone else, we can be tempted to hide from each other, to disappear. Sometimes we are tempted to run away completely. There are times when removing oneself is appropriate, as a matter of safety. When we are not safe, we should remove ourselves from the situation. We also can be tempted to disappear when our safety isn't in jeopardy but we have been offended. We harden our hearts.

Before we act on those impulses, we may want to ask ourselves what we may lose if we run away from each other when an offense is committed. In an interview on National Public Radio, the Rev. Nadia Bolz-Weber, pastor of House for All Sinners and Saints in Denver, made the point well. She tells everyone at Sinners and Saints that we will miss the power and transformation that can come with reconciliation if we leave the moment we are offended or disappointed.[5]

Seminary is the place to practice and to experiment with staying in relationship when things becoming difficult and challenging. We can practice learning to soften toward others when they offend us, rather than hardening our hearts toward them. As we do, we not only open ourselves up to the power of God's grace but also prepare ourselves for ministerial leadership when we will need to help others soften their hearts.

Sabbath

Remembering the Sabbath is probably the most neglected commandment.[6] Our lives are filled with invitations to do, to be, and to have more. Being available at all times is a higher priority than the quality of presence that comes with having time for rest. Being busy has become an American virtue, suggesting success and self-realization. Overworking is a badge of honor.

While some strands of Christianity have interpreted this commandment to apply to Christians differently from the way it applies to the Jewish community, there is still agreement that Christians are expected to stop working and to rest each week. By committing ourselves to resting on a regular basis, we remind ourselves and others that the future, including our own, does not rest in our hands alone. Through our ceasing to work, we not only provide sustenance to our beings but also acknowledge God's presence and engagement with the world. Our refusal to stop pushing, to stop producing, to stop laboring is as much a theological statement as it is a social one. In his book *Sabbath: Restoring the Sacred Rhythm of Rest*, Wayne Muller makes the striking claim that

> [p]oisoned by this hypnotic belief that good things come only through unceasing determination and tireless effort, we can never truly rest. And for want of rest, our lives are in danger.
>
> In our drive for success we are seduced by the promises of more: more money, more recognition, more satisfaction, more love, more information, more influence, more possessions, more security. Even when our intentions are noble and our efforts sincere—even when we dedicate our lives to the service of others—the corrosive pressure of frantic overactivity can nonetheless cause suffering in ourselves and others.
>
> A "successful" life has become a violent enterprise.[7]

Muller isn't suggesting that work isn't important or valuable. The issue is the false belief that we can sustain our own lives through our own labors. To believe this is to follow the path of destruction of ourselves and others. The stakes are high when we refuse to keep

Sabbath, whether that is setting aside a day, an afternoon, or an hour on a regular basis to pause, to breathe, and to quiet our lives.

Keeping Sabbath while in seminary is important. It becomes increasingly difficult to practice, especially if you have family commitments and need to keep your job. We can be tempted to think that we can continue to add more and more responsibilities to our lives without any consequences. That isn't true. We are limited beings with a limited amount of time and energy.

Every year I ask new students, "What will you let go of when you begin your theology studies?" Each student has at least one activity or commitment that they need to set aside in order to pursue their degree. Most of them have several. No one can make the decisions for you about which commitments and activities you need to pause or stop. Each person needs to determine what balance looks like in his or her life. Most of us will need help too. We need the support and wisdom of others to know when we need to slow down.

Every year I have students come to my office, presenting a variety of issues and looking for guidance. Some say that they need to be mentored in how to do theological research and writing. Some begin by sharing problems they are experiencing with their family members. One even shared that he was being mean with the family dog. In each case my job is to help them identify the underlying issue. The presenting problem is often not the real issue but a symptom of the real issue. The most common challenge is that students are trying to do too much. They are working in a job full-time, taking care of their family, serving in their congregation in some capacity, and trying to take a full-time credit load. It's no wonder they are struggling with their studies. They have no time to do all the academic work, let alone rest. This is what Muller means when he says, "A 'successful' life has become a violent enterprise."

Keeping Sabbath won't become easier after graduation. It will remain a challenge, because there will always be good things, good people, and good events looking for your attention. The time to remember the Sabbath is now. Learn its graces through practicing it while you are in school. Allow the time of rest to open you to the presence of the Holy Spirit all around you. If taking an entire day is too much for you to claim, begin with a few hours or an afternoon each week. It isn't time to run errands or to complete nonschool tasks. It's time to allow your body and spirit to be calm. You don't need to go anywhere special or to have any special prayer gadgets. Take a walk in the park. Curl up with a cup of coffee and a favorite book. Play with your children. There are endless ways in which we can take time for Sabbath each day and each week. When you return to your school work, you will be more relaxed and more able to do the work that you need to do.

FRIENDSHIP AND FAMILY

Friendship is a powerful aspect of seminary life. The amount of time seminarians spend together in class and with other curricular activities is one reason this is the case, but the main reason is the shared experience of learning how to theologize. Seminarians are learning new vocabulary and testing new worldviews. There is a power unleashed in a classroom and community when people explore together important ideas that have shaped the life of the world. These ideas have enough energy to change the ways people think about themselves and their place in the world. They can change the ways they think about God and the role of religion in the world. Consequently, seminarians develop meaningful bonds that often last a lifetime.

These friendships, however, need cultivation and attention. Seminarians need to spend time with others and to take the risk of becoming vulnerable if they want friendship to flourish. Some may find this invitation unappealing or even scary. My experience is that any liabilities that come with being open to friendship are worth it.[8]

Family members of seminarians can have a variety of experiences and responses to seminary. Some family members will not support a decision to enter seminary, usually because they have concerns about the family member pursuing ordained ministry. Parents, grandparents, spouses, siblings, and children can have reservations about ministry for numerous reasons. What's most important at the beginning stages is to get those conversations started as soon as possible. Each objection and relationship needs to be taken seriously, but they can't determine necessarily the process or the outcome.

Spousal relationships are the ones that deserve ongoing attention. If someone discerns a call to ministry after making a spousal commitment, the one called to ministry bears the responsibility of making sure that all the factors and implications of this invitation are discussed. Pursuing a theology degree is a commitment that involves the time, the economic resources, and the emotional resources of the entire family, not just of the seminarian. In addition, pursuing a life of ministry involves the entire family. Spouses, parents, and children are all affected by a decision to pursue a call to ordained ministry. In all cases the commitment is life changing. In some cases it's severe. For example, some denominations reassign clergy every three years. While the new assignment will be within a limited geographic range, it will still likely require a change in schools for children and the moving of the family household. This practice is called the itinerant system. Military families experience a similar practice.

Seminarians shouldn't wait until their spouses voice concerns about the implications for a life of ordained ministry. Instead, they should be proactive with their spouses about exploring options that are available to them. Even when spouses completely support the decision to enter ministry, there will still be changes in daily life that will need to be discussed. Children or the plan to have children will also have an impact on the decision to pursue seminary and ordained ministry.

It's not unusual for seminarians to experience discord with their spouses and children. The seminarian is experiencing a theological and spiritual adventure that she or he is sharing with classmates. The friendship and camaraderie that emerge in that adventure are beautiful and life giving. They can also be threatening to spouses and children. Spouses can feel left behind as the seminarian experiences a growth in faith. Children, depending on their age, need to adjust to the idea of being children of a pastor. For some children, this is a nonevent; for others, it feels like an incredible burden. Other clergy people and their spouses can be valuable resources for seminarians and new clergy families. The spouses of other seminarians can also be a valuable resource. If your seminary doesn't have a support group for the spouses of seminarians and new clergy, consider proposing one to student services at the seminary. If your spouse is looking for support, there are likely other spouses looking for support too.

When spouses or children have difficulty adapting to the changes in family life that come with seminary and ministry, it's important to seek outside help. Some seminaries have chaplains or a dean of students who can provide assistance for seminarians and their families. All seminaries will know of local resources and can make referrals. Don't hesitate to reach out for help. You won't be the first family to struggle with the assorted adjustments that come with being a clergy family.

THERAPY AND COUNSELING

All of us come into a professional degree program in theological studies with wounds. There are the wounds that we have received and the wounds that we have inflicted. There are also numerous memories, relationships, and experiences, both beautiful and tender, that we hold as we contemplate the relationship between God and the universe. Each part of our history remains alive within us. Digging deeper into the theological categories and acts of grace, sin, redemption, mercy, love, forgiveness, resurrection, restitution, and hope is bound to lay bare aspects of our personal lives that need additional attention. This isn't necessarily because we didn't deal with the issues earlier. We may have done all that we could do and needed to do regarding an event in our lives, but now that experience needs more investigation and understanding.

Seminary faculties expect that theology programs will cause issues to surface in students, issues that need to be addressed if the student intends to make satisfactory progress toward the degree and her or his vocational goal. When these occasions arise, it's healthy and wise to seek out the help of mental-health professionals. Seminarians don't need the permission of the seminary to pursue counseling or therapy, but seminary staff and faculty involved with student services will be able to make appropriate referrals. In some cases the seminary will have a negotiated rate for seminarians who do not have insurance to cover the expense.

There are also moments in which the faculty will suggest or require a student to seek out professional counseling. This can happen for a variety of reasons, such as disruptive behavior in the classroom or other activities, depletion of energy, episodes of depression, lack of self-awareness, unsatisfactory academic progress, and violation of standards.

Most of the time a seminarian is able to address the issue while continuing in the degree program. The therapy sessions may necessitate a reduction in course load, but the trade-off is worth the progress that the student can make when he or she has the time to deal with the emerging issue. There are moments, however, when the issue that has surfaced is so significant that a student needs to take a leave of absence. The difficulties from the problem can be so emotionally disturbing and destabilizing that it's not possible for the student to concentrate on studying or doing field work. I have worked with numerous students who have found themselves in this place. No matter how disappointing it is, taking a leave of absence or even withdrawing from a program is much wiser than trying to push through the program. Ignoring the issues will not work. They will eventually surface and could cause even greater pain. Once the issues have been addressed, the student can request to return to the program.

FAILURE, STRUGGLE, AND RESILIENCY

Struggle and failure are not necessarily bad. Indeed, there are times when they are destructive to us and to others. Most of the time, however, they can be important occasions for growth. Struggling to understand an author, writing a failing paper, or preaching a poor sermon tells us where we need to invest our energy and attention. It reveals to us the limits of our thinking, our language, and our ability to communicate. All of us are bound to fail at some point. In fact, one of the intended outcomes of a professional degree in theological studies is for students to know their limits and the ways in which they can work to move beyond them.

Having a healthy sense of struggle and failure also develops resilience in us. Without experiencing trials, difficulties, or defeats we will not develop the resiliency needed for ministerial leadership. Congregations and communities need leaders who can withstand challenges and setbacks. They need people who will remain committed to a mission even when there are forces working at cross purposes. They need leaders who can help the congregation develop that same kind of resiliency. Stamina and resiliency need to be cultivated. They don't develop on their own.

BEING HUMAN, BEING CHRISTIAN

Before we start thinking about what we need to do and be as a leader, we need to figure out what we think it means to be a human and what it means to be a Christian. Without those two things, we won't be able to lead others along the path of Christian discipleship. We won't know how to support others with the joys, challenges, and disappointments of discipleship if we haven't sought to understand them for ourselves. Christian theologizing has something to contribute to all disciplines and areas of study, but it has something particular to say about what it means to be human.

This is all to say that the identify-formation apprenticeship, which is prevalent in the MDiv degree but present in all theology degrees to some extent, scopes out its primary territory in the areas of Christian anthropology, spirituality, and discipleship. Participants in this apprenticeship confront their identity as human beings, including all the glories and limitations that entails. They probe the breadth of human wretchedness, making what peace they can with the reality that all of us are capable of humanity's worst acts. They also encounter the reality of the sociality of human sinfulness. There are no innocent bystanders. All of us contribute in some way to the downfall of others and the world.

In the same breath, participants encounter the power of God's grace and love in their lives. They learn how to identify the paschal mystery of living, dying, and rising in their own existence. Having been baptized into Christ, they join Christ in this beautiful redemptive passage. As they befriend their human frailties and limitations, they discover these as opportunities to experience God's desire for human flourishing. This experience of grace offered to them at the most undeserved of moments has the potential to soften their hearts. By taking their humanity seriously, seminarians discover what it means to be people of faith who rely on the grace of God and not on human self-righteousness.

The identity-formation apprenticeship is a school of discipleship. Those who graduate should be ready to accompany others along the path of discipleship. They should be secure when faced with the sinfulness of others, regardless of whether they are repentant. They should be temperate in their assessment of others. Most of all, they should be eager and wise to discern with others how God is calling them to a deeper and wider way of living.

ADDITIONAL READING

Barry, William A. and William J. Connolly. *The Practice of Spiritual Direction.* 2nd ed., revised. New York: HarperCollins, 2009.

Cameron, Julia. *The Artist's Way.* New York: Putnam, 2002.

Goldberg, Natalie. *Writing Down the Bones: Freeing the Writer Within.* 2nd ed. Boston: Shambala, 2005.

Muller, Wayne. *Sabbath: Restoring the Sacred Rhythm of Rest.* New York: Bantam, 1999.

Weems, Renita J. *Listening for God: A Minister's Journey through Silence and Doubt.* New York: Simon and Schuster, 1999.

7

Learning While Pastoring

Pastor Kevin has had his weekly staff meeting on Wednesday morning at ten o'clock for the past ten years. In August he announced that the meeting would now move to Wednesday afternoon at one o'clock, because he has Introduction to the Old Testament on Wednesday mornings until noon at the seminary. His commute between the church and the seminary is forty-five minutes when traffic is in his favor. He plans to eat his lunch in the car while he is driving. He lets his staff know that the schedule will likely change each semester for the next several years, depending on his class schedule. Pastor Kevin quickly realizes that his decision to enter seminary will have an impact on his congregation and church staff. It will affect his family even more.

Arriving at seminary after serving for a time as a pastor is a common occurrence. For many denominations, a call to ministry is an act of the Holy Spirit and not contingent on engaging programmatic theological education. Other denominations have a history of establishing student pastors. In these cases a student is assigned to pastor a church while she or he pursues theological education, either in a degree program at a seminary or in a denominational certificate program.

In some cases, pastors will apply to a seminary degree program after many years of church leadership experience. At some point in their ministry, these pastors have become aware of a real need to deepen their spiritual life, increase their leadership skills, and expand their theological thinking. In other cases, pastors will arrive at the seminary because their denomination has strongly encouraged them to seek formal theological training for the benefit of the church's ministry. Regardless of the situation, serving as pastor while doing a graduate theological degree is demanding.

Pastoring while being a student creates exciting opportunities for the pastor, the pastor's family, and the pastor's congregation. It also presents significant challenges and stresses. In this chapter we look at the opportunities and the challenges and explore ideas to help make the educational experience as feasible and generative as possible.

CLAIMING TIME AND SPACE

In chapter 2 we discussed the importance of all your life commitments and how they impact the amount of time you will really have to devote to your seminary program. Once you have decided to enroll in a program, you'll need to take steps to set aside the necessary time to do the work. You'll also need to identify where you will be able to study. This process is not done alone but in dialogue and cooperation with one's family and ministerial setting. The pastor may be attending seminary, but everyone has the potential to be affected.

Time

If you are going to succeed in your program, you will need to make changes in your schedule, reduce the number of other commitments, and seek the help and cooperation of family members and coworkers. The more commitments you have in your life, the more challenging it will be and the more adjustments you may need to make. There isn't a simple equation, because every student's situation is different. Some students are working in a full-time job, ministering in their church, and raising children. Other students have only one of these commitments. Some students have none of them. Depending on the details of your particular life, you may need to set aside even more time. For example, if you need to commute to your classes, you'll need to build commuting time into your calculations. With advance planning, a disciplined use of time, and the cooperation of family and coworkers, you can make this work.

The first step is to take an inventory of all your commitments and how much time you spend daily, weekly, and yearly on these commitments.

Map out on paper or on computer your commitments. Begin with a typical week in your life, filling in each day. Then do a map of an entire year. If you have special annual commitments—such as a family reunion, summer camp, house chores, or church conference—be sure to put them on the calendar.

Once you have a clear picture of how you currently spend your time, you can begin to block out the space you will need for classes, study time, and other seminary requirements like worship, conferences, and cross-cultural trips. How much time you will need for class and for study will be affected by what type of class you are taking (fully online, hybrid, or fully residential), your study habits, and your academic skills. The professor is responsible for communicating how much time is expected to complete the requirements of the course. You, however, may need more or less time and should plan accordingly.

After combining into one calendar the various courses, other degree requirements, and your previous commitments, you will quickly see where there may be conflicts. *Expect to find conflicts in your schedule.* It's impossible to add a graduate-degree program to your life and not have them. This means that you'll need to decide what you must set aside and what you can simplify while you are pursuing your degree. There is no single or right answer to this question. Everyone has to set something aside in order to create the time needed to complete the degree. And everyone needs to find ways to simplify some of the basic patterns of life.

One helpful way to approach this process is to explore what it means for you to live a balanced life and what assumptions you have about what balance means. You may have to recalibrate your daily expectations. You may not be able to exercise every day for the ideal amount of time. You may not be able to cook a homemade meal every night. You may not be able to spend as much time with friends and family every day. You may not be able to clean your house or apartment as often as you have in the past. Each person will need to decide what a balanced life will look like during this period of academic study.

Here are a few things you may want to consider as you create the space you need for your seminary degree program:

— Can I simplify my food preparation and eating, without jeopardizing my health?
— Can I simplify my clothing options so that I can spend less time on clothing care and decisions about what to wear?
— Can I get another type of haircut that requires less time?

—Is there someone in my family who can help me or my family with childcare, housecleaning, or laundry?

—Can I reduce the amount of time driving by combining errands with commuting?

—Can I find other ways or times to exercise without jeopardizing my health?

—What commitments at church can I set down? What committees or leadership responsibilities can I relinquish?

—What projects at home can be postponed or taken up by another member of the family?

—What forms of recreation (e.g., computer games, travel, sporting events, television) can I set aside or engage in less often?

—What adjustments must I make in order to spend time with my immediate and extended family? What advance planning must I do to ensure I spend time with family?

—Is there any extra work or overtime that I can eliminate from my job?

Even if you make adjustments in your personal schedule as you begin your program, you may need to make more as you get further into the process. Students in a master of divinity program or in one of the other professional degree programs will be expected to do field education in addition to taking courses. This change normally includes an increase in work, travel time, and expense. When this happens, a student may need to cut back even further for the length of the field-education covenant. Students may be required to work in a different church or institution, taking them away from their home church on a Sunday or during the week. While this is a standard practice in theological schools and most churches will be expecting this, it still requires some advance planning on your part and significant schedule changes.

Study Space

You'll need a space where you will be able to focus on your reading, studying, reflecting, and writing. You'll also need Internet access and room to shelve your books.

You may want or need to use your current office at home or at work. That makes perfect sense. The challenge is helping others to know when you can't be disturbed. If your congregation has a culture where people can walk into your office anytime you are there, it may be hard to get the quiet time you need. In some cases, all you need to do is to hang a "Do Not Disturb" sign on the door and let your assistant know not to interrupt unless there is an emergency. Putting an automatic responder on your email works well too. Letting people know that you are not available to respond to them immediately helps to manage their expectations. It also releases you from any compulsion to be tied to your email or cell phone.

Carving out study time and space at home can be equally challenging. Family members may expect you to be available as long as you are home, regardless of whether you need to do homework. If you are working from home, you may need to help family members to recalibrate their expectations for your availability. Establish study hours when you can close the office door and work without interruption.

In my experience, studying at the graduate level requires more significant changes in one's home and work space. You'll likely need to use your work spaces at times when people are not likely to demand your attention. Some students work late at night; others wake up early in the morning in order to get studying done before anyone else is out of bed.

Many students simply cannot study in a home or work office. There are too many distractions, internally and externally. In these cases, you may want to use a library, coffee shop, or other quiet location that has Internet access. You will have to carry around your books and computer all the time, but it will be worth it if you can do your work.

Don't be timid about doing what it takes to have the study space that you need for your education. If you can work well and efficiently in that space, you'll save time that you can spend with your family and friends.

Beyond carving out the study time and space that you need, it's important to share regularly with your family members, coworkers, and congregants about why it's important that you take the time you need for your education. We explore this in more detail later in this chapter.

MOVING BETWEEN PASTOR AND STUDENT

Being a pastor and a graduate student at the same time demands good time-management skills, but it also requires other skills. Depending on the institution and the particular degree program, pastors who become seminary students may need to practice changing roles when they enter a theological degree program. In their congregational or ministerial setting, they are expected to provide leadership and guiding language for the work of the community or institution. In the classroom, however, they have a different role. They are students, interacting with a group of seminarian peers, of whom some are pastors and others have just graduated from college. Their role in the classroom is to be students, not pastors. This may be the most challenging part of being a student and pastor at the same time. If the pastor is ministering in a theological tradition that expects the pastor to be the theological authority in the congregation, then it is often disorienting and confusing to her or him to move into a classroom setting where the student is asked to bracket that authority, for the sake of allowing everyone the opportunity to explore a variety of perspectives. Pastoring students find themselves needing to adjust their voices every time they move between their congregation and the seminary.

Seminarians—both those who are pastoring and those who are not—are often not aware of this dynamic until some disagreement arises in the classroom. For example, the students could be discussing a particular aspect of Christian theology and find themselves differing not only in perspective but also in the solidity of their perspective. The pastoring student may arrive at the discussion with a very clear viewpoint, while the inexperienced student may be very unclear about what he or she thinks. In these cases, it's important that there is space for everyone to do the exploration that he or she needs to do. The course instructor is responsible for creating this space, but the fruitfulness of it relies on the thoughtfulness and work of the students.

Students with little pastoral experience can benefit from what the pastoring students know about dealing with various theological issues in a community. The students who have been pastoring for years have wisdom to offer in the classroom. It's also true that the pastoring students can benefit from those who are coming into the conversations with fresh eyes and ears. Their pastoral experience may be limited, but they can bring to the table new questions that aren't burdened by previous disappointments and limitations.

Pastoring students will often report experiencing some relief when they step into the seminary classroom, because they are granted permission not to know all the answers to every theological and spiritual challenge. These students relish the fact that in the seminary classroom they don't have to be experts or authorities in theology, the

Bible, or church matters. In these moments they can allow themselves to be students and colearners with their peers. In this learning environment they can also experiment with or practice ideas and perspectives before introducing them into their pastoral practice.

In other cases, pastoring students will report experiencing distress when learning how to approach theology from an academic perspective. These students can be quick to identify theological ideas or biblical interpretations that are not compatible with those held in their pastoral settings. When these divergences appear, pastoring students must remember that it's the responsibility of the spiritual leader to carefully consider a variety of theological ideas, practices, and traditions in the pursuit of wisdom. The invitation is to set aside the question about whether something is immediately applicable in the local context, until the student has had the chance to digest the information for herself or himself.

As the pastoring student gets deeper and deeper into her or his studies, these divergences in theological matters are likely to increase, thereby increasing the stress of moving back and forth between being a student and being a pastor. This is completely normal and to be expected. In fact, I would think most seminaries would be very disturbed if a pastoring student, or any other student, didn't experience some dissonance in the educational process. Studying theology in an academic setting requires exploring critically long-held beliefs about God, humanity, church, world, salvation, knowledge, and power. As discussed in chapter 6, a theological education necessitates moving beyond any naiveté we may have about being a person of faith and a spiritual leader. For some pastors—not all—this process can be very destabilizing. Beliefs and practices that have been sustaining personally and ministerially may be called into question. When this happens, the pastor must use the critical skills developed in the program to arrive at a new place. New relationships with the Bible, God, church, and world will emerge.

FIELD EDUCATION

For those pastors in a master of divinity degree program, field education can be complicated. All MDiv programs require field education or supervised ministry, usually the equivalent of four semesters. The assumption is that theological students benefit from apprenticing with a more seasoned practitioner. When the student is already pastoring, the supervisory aspect of the requirement becomes awkward. In addition, some pastors—but not all of them—are supervised by a regional pastor, elder, superintendent, or bishop. In some cases the pastor reports to elders or the board of the local church.

The temptation would be to request that the seminary waive the field-education requirement for the student because of her or his position. Such a request would probably not be approved and could reflect poorly on the student. Such a request suggests to the seminary that the student isn't open to learning or to being supervised.

Instead, consider how this part of the curriculum could be helpful. Where do you need to grow as a minister? What skills do you need to develop? Solicit input from leaders in your congregation or ministry setting. Ask them for ideas. Tell them that this is part of your degree program and that you want to use your field-education requirement to become a stronger spiritual leader. Some student pastors have used field education to strengthen their preaching. Others have used it to develop stronger pastoral-care skills, administrative skills, stewardship skills, or strategic-planning skills.

Once you have identified the areas where you want to grow, you can begin working with the seminary to find the appropriate supervisor and to put together the learning covenant. The supervisor could be another pastor in the area who is skilled in the areas where you want to grow or improve. The supervisor could also be a bishop, regional pastor, elder, or superintendent. If your denomination has assigned you a mentor, that person may be able to be your supervisor. In addition to being approved by the seminary, the supervisor has to be a person whom you trust and who has the time and desire to work with you. The field-education supervisor is often involved in the formation-assessment process of the seminary, so it's important that you are comfortable with this person and that there is no conflict of interest.[1]

Ideally, you would spend part or half of your field-education requirement in a setting outside your ministerial setting. If you are working in a congregation, consider working in a nonprofit organization that does direct service to those in need. No matter how much experience you have in pastoral ministry, providing direct service to the hungry, the thirsty, the homeless, the refugee is important, transforming work. If you work in a nonprofit organization as your vocation, consider working in a congregation or another type of nonprofit. Stepping outside our normal ministry context interrupts our assumptions about what ministry and spiritual leadership can look like.

If you haven't experienced clinical pastoral education (CPE), I strongly recommend that you investigate doing one unit of CPE to fulfill part of your field-education requirement.[2] Many schools will allow you to replace the equivalent of two semesters of field education with one unit of CPE. Because CPE is such an intense experience, you'll need to take a close look at your home, school, and work schedule. Concentrated units are equivalent to working full-time. Extended units of CPE may require eight to ten hours of service each week. You'll need more time beyond this, however, to process what you have experienced. If you are doing CPE, you'll likely need to review and reduce all your other commitments at work and school.

FAMILY LIFE

All seminarians who have family obligations will need to pay attention to how enrolling in seminary impacts their family members. Earlier in this chapter we explored the reality of needing time and space for your studies. What's important to add here is that a seminarian with a family will feel the pull of multiple commitments and claims. Making sure that the lines of communication are open between you and your family members is crucial. If you are a parent, your studies will require you to spend less time with your children or at least to rearrange the time that you spend with them. There will be times when you will disappoint a family member because you won't be able to do everything that you did before you began your degree program. You'll feel disappointed too.

Consequently, it is important to schedule family time and vacation time. Whether or not you still have assignment deadlines, when those family times arrive, do your family and yourself a favor and allow yourself to take time off to enjoy the time you have with your family. If you make good on your commitments to spend time together, you'll all be freer to accept the moments when your studies prevent you from spending time together.

Seeing less of you is not the only way family members are impacted by your decision to enter seminary. As you move through the program, you'll be inspired, confused, relieved, discouraged, and hopeful. You'll be having many conversations with many new people: colleagues, professors, and classmates. You'll be talking about things that matter to you deeply. Every week you will be introduced to new ways of seeing God and the world! You'll also be learning new theological terms and new ways of thinking theologically.

Seminary is a very exciting and meaningful experience. But your family members will experience very little of what you experience. They won't be in class. They may not meet many of your classmates or professors. They may not see anything that you present in class. When they do hear you teach, preach, and speak, they'll notice the changes in your vocabulary and in your theological worldview.

Not every family member may be as excited as you are about all your new experiences, friendships, and ideas. Some will be thrilled and will ask you to share with them what you are learning. They may ask to read what you are reading. Some will want to meet your classmates and professors. Others, however, may feel left out. They may even resent the time and energy you are spending on school work and the relationships that you are developing. It's possible that some of them won't be interested in what you are learning or will find it boring.

Whether or not your family members are as enthusiastic as you are about your studies, all of them will need to adjust to the ways that a theological education will change you. You'll be revising the ways that you see the world, God, humanity, and the church. The evolution in your thinking and attitudes will make sense to you because you will be spending so much time paying attention to those changes. But your family members aren't doing all that work. If they want to follow what you are learning or to participate more actively, you'll need to consider how to include them in the process.

If you want to include one or more family members in your educational process, it would be helpful to distinguish between sharing the ideas and perspectives presented in the program and sharing *how you are experiencing* those ideas and perspectives, theologically and spiritually. In most cases you would talk about both; but making sure that you differentiate between them will help you and your family members. It will reinforce the important point that, no matter what you study, read, or discover, there is still room for you to decide what you will believe and why. Because your family members aren't in the program, they may not understand why it's important to examine multiple perspectives in the process of theological reflection. They may find it confusing. That's why it's also important to share with them where you are theologically and spiritually, as you investigate and ponder such a variety of big ideas, viewpoints, and traditions.

Another option for including a spouse in your education process is to invite your spouse to join you in taking a course. Some seminaries have a provision that allows a spouse to audit a limited number of courses with his or her seminarian spouse. Auditors are required to do all the reading but not the other assignments. Having this shared experience will allow your spouse to understand more about what you are learning and how it impacts your theological worldview and practice.

CONGREGATIONAL LIFE

Much of what can be said about family members and their responses to your theological education can be extended to congregations and their members. Some congregations and members will be excited and proud that their pastor has entered a seminary degree program. Others will disapprove, saying that a theological degree isn't necessary or that it will change the pastor too much. Still others will be afraid that the pastor won't want to stay in their church after she or he finishes the degree. These responses are common, whether the pastor is doing a master's degree or a doctoral degree in theological studies.

Regardless of how a congregation or individual members respond, it's worth considering how you can include your congregation in your educational process. You'll want to do it thoughtfully and carefully. Otherwise, you can create more difficulties for yourself and your congregation.

Most theological students, pastors or not, are tempted to take ideas that they have learned in the classroom and to share them immediately in their pastoral context. New information regarding matters of consequence—like God, church, world, and humanity—generates serious energy. Students intuit this even if they don't always know the reason why. Theological education, however, isn't a matter of delivering information. It's about what happens when human beings engage in deep, critical reflection on human existence, our origin, our future, our life together, and the God who we believe animates all reality. The questions and discussions that arise from this process aren't always welcome, comfortable, or peaceful. For those who aren't prepared, they can be psychologically and spiritually dangerous.

Pastoring seminarians should think twice before repeating in their pastoral context theological ideas or biblical perspectives learned in class.[3] Instead, it may be more helpful to your congregation and to you to share some of the questions that doctrinal theologians, biblical scholars, church historians, and practical theologians ask themselves. The general themes of these questions will not likely be new to you or others. But as you go deeper into your studies, you will be able to ask more nuanced and complex questions. For example, in addition to asking congregants, "How do you imagine God?" you can ask them, "Where do our metaphors for God come from?" "What do you make of the fact that the Bible has multiple metaphors for God?" "How do you respond viscerally to the various metaphors for God?"

If you invite members of your congregation to join you in wrestling with some of the basic questions that inspire theological studies, you'll be better prepared for seminary classroom discussions, and your congregants will be able to join you in the educational process. Focusing on the fundamental questions won't guarantee that everyone will be as excited as you about studying theology or will be as appreciative of the process. Some people will be unsettled by the questions and their implications. Consequently, you'll want to consider the best forum in which to share them. Some may work fine in a sermon. Others will be better suited for Sunday school, adult education, or a committee meeting. Finally, if you are able to include your congregation in your theological studies in this way, you'll be able to lessen the stress of switching roles between pastor and student. You'll discover with your congregants that being a person of faith is always a matter of being a student. We all have more to learn.

THE GRACE OF BEING A PASTORING STUDENT

Many of the challenges that a pastoring student faces are similar to those experienced by other seminarians. Shifting theological views, time constraints, financial pressures, and competing demands are part of what it means to be a seminarian today. Most seminarians won't have the privilege of entering seminary right after college, debt free, free of family obligations, and without a need to work at the same time.

On the other hand, there are some challenges that are specific to the pastoring student. The biggest challenge is changing roles as one goes back and forth between the congregation and the seminary classroom. This reality can be emotionally and spiritually challenging. As noted above, there are ways to connect being a pastor and being a theology student that can mitigate the need to constantly switch roles.

There are graces that come with already being a pastor on entering seminary. Two come to mind. The first is that pastoring students are freed from thinking of a theological education as a hoop that they need to jump through in order to get to ordination or ministerial authorization. Unfortunately, some students who come from traditions that require a theological degree before ordination treat the degree program as something to endure until they can be authorized for ministry. If you are already ordained, you don't have that pressure.

The second grace is related to the first. Pastoring students may appreciate more deeply the freedom to explore the diversity of theological worldviews. Because they are already pastoring, they don't have the pressure to articulate a complete theological position by the time they graduate. Instead, they can see the degree program for what it is: an opportunity to gather skills, information, and practices that will support a lifetime of theological reflection and growth.

ADDITIONAL READING

Barton, Ruth Haley. *Strengthening the Soul of Your Leadership: Seeking God in the Crucible of Ministry.* Downers Grove, IL: InterVarsity, 2008.
Farber-Robertson, Anita, with M. B. Handspicker and Rabbi David Whiman. *Learning While Leading: Increasing Your Effectiveness in Ministry.* Bethesda, MD: Alban Institute, 2000.

8

The Job-Search Process

Historically, students would begin looking for a ministerial position during their final year of seminary studies. Today, however, ministerial transitions can take place at any time. And the search process can take eighteen months or more, depending on the type of position you are seeking. Some students are already authorized for ministry and already serving. They can experience a change in assignment in the middle of their studies. A church, agency, or institution can encounter a budget crisis that requires a change in staffing. Other students can be called into ministry before they have completed their degree. A denominational leader may need to assign a new pastor and decide to approach a seminarian about filling the position. A church, agency, or institution can be so impressed with the work of a seminarian while she or he is doing field education that they approach the student about taking a position before graduation. This all means that part of being a professional religious leader means always being ready for a change in assignments.

The job-search process for ministers has a lot in common with search processes for other types of positions. There are, however, a number of differences. This chapter will address those elements that are specific to people looking for ministry or ministry-related positions. We'll also highlight some best practices that pertain to the job-search process in general.

Some seminarians belong to a denomination that assigns clergy or clergy candidates to a congregation or position. The clergy person may have some voice in that process; in other cases the decision rests solely in the hands of a bishop or other denominational leader. Sometimes a congregation will be allowed to pick from a selection of two or three candidates. If you belong to a denomination where you are assigned to a congregation or position, it will still be helpful to read this chapter and note the types of things that are learned and negotiated in other processes. The process is still a professional one, and there are always elements that can be or need to be negotiated.

If you are not assigned and need to locate opportunities yourself, before you begin looking, spend some time identifying your ideal type of position. In fact, it is helpful to prioritize options. What would be your first choice, your ideal position? What would be your second choice? What about your third? Clarifying your desires will help you to focus your energy. At the beginning you'll want to focus only on your first choice. If you find that you aren't finding good matches, expand your circle of interest to include the second tier. Expand again to include the third tier, if needed. Many job seekers get so consumed with getting a position that they lose focus and lose time applying for positions that they really don't want. Don't begin the process by settling for a position that won't be a good fit for you or the organization.

Once you have prioritized your list of possibilities, start looking for a position. Find out where job openings for your ideal position are posted. If you want to work at a nonprofit organization, contact places where you would like to work and inquire. Even if they don't have an opening at the moment, they are always keeping their eye out for applicants with potential. Find out if they would welcome a letter and CV or résumé from you.

If you are looking for a position as a pastor and are not assigned, your denomination will have a protocol for you to follow. Study those instructions carefully and follow them. Many denominations now have online systems that help clergy assemble important employment and vocational documents, called profiles. The profiles are designed to help congregations find candidates and to help candidates find congregations.

Profiles don't replace the need for ministers to keep track of their achievements, completed projects, sermons, evaluations, and other information. On enrolling in a seminary program, all students should begin preparing for the job-application process and all upcoming ministerial transitions. If you track and organize what you experience and produce during seminary, you'll have a much easier time when you need to seek employment.

PORTFOLIOS

Portfolios have become a popular and convenient way for seminarians and ministers to catalog important artifacts that demonstrate their performance and quality of work. Other professions have been using portfolios for centuries. For example, illustrators, sketch artists, and painters assemble specific selections of their work to share with potential employers, investors, or clients. The portfolio changes, depending on type of presentation the artist is making. A minister should also have a catalog of works, usually called artifacts, that could be assembled in different ways for different audiences.

Many seminaries and other educational institutions have begun requiring all students to have a portfolio of their work. Academic institutions need to collect a sampling of student work for accreditation purposes. Often schools will collect one student artifact from every required course. This artifact is stored in the student's portfolio, where both the student and the school can access the file. Some of the software programs even allow the faculty member to grade the paper inside the portfolio, sharing comments with the student. In addition, the student can elect to share those faculty comments with potential employers. Of course, the student needs to think carefully about what artifacts and comments he or she wants to share.

Most e-portfolio programs provide graduates with access to their artifacts and portfolios for several years after graduation. When the agreement expires, the graduate will have the option to extend the service for an annual fee. If you decide not to extend the service, be sure to keep copies of all your artifacts in your own electronic files. There is a benefit, however, to maintaining the subscription to an e-portfolio program. You can file important documents that mark your professional abilities and development, and you can give people access to those artifacts when you find it helpful. In the years to come, you may want to refer back to an early sermon or essay, looking for how your worldview has changed over time. Another option is to create your own website and store your artifacts on the website. The downside of this option is that you have everything posted for everyone to see. A portfolio program is designed for you to share your work in strategic ways.

Artifacts

Regardless of which artifacts your seminary may require you to save in your portfolio, you need to make your own plans. You should have at least one artifact in each of these categories:

— Preached sermon manuscript (This could come from a course, field education, or another event.)
— Preached sermon video recording (This could come from a course, field education, or another event. It should be a different sermon from the manuscript artifact.)
— Preaching evaluations (This could come from a course, field education, or another event.)
— Orders of worship (These should be ones that you created and used.)
— Curriculum plan or proposal (The topic should be related to the type of ministry you intend to do.)
— Biblical interpretation work (This could come from a Bible course and should demonstrate your exegetical skills.)
— Original pastoral-care case study or verbatim (This could come from a CPE experience or doing pastoral care in another setting.)
— Theology and philosophy-of-ministry statement (Most seminaries will require this at some point in the program.)
— Philosophy of teaching statement (Your religious education course will likely require such a statement.)
— Theology and worldview statement (Most seminaries will require this at some point in the program.)
— Field education/supervised ministry evaluations
— Clinical pastoral education (CPE) final evaluation

When reviewed together, the body of artifacts should give the reader or potential employer a clear sense of what you believe about God, the church, humanity, and the world. The exact points that you should be sure to cover in your ministry statement, teaching statement, and theology/worldview statement will vary, depending on your institutional commitments and intended ministry. Here are a few questions to stimulate your reflection:

— What is your understanding and experience of God? What ideas, commitments, and experiences shape this understanding? How do you image God? How has this image developed or changed over time?

—What authorities (e.g., sacred texts, personal experiences, traditions, church laws) do you consult, accept, or submit to in shaping your theological views? To what extent do these conform to or challenge those generally accepted by your denomination or ordaining body?

—How do you understand humanity? How would you describe our deepest needs and our human condition? What is sin and how would you describe its dynamics?[1]

If you are unclear about which topics should be covered in your statements, contact the person or committee in your denomination that is in charge of approving ordained ministers. They should be able to share with you what the denomination is expecting from an applicant for authorized ministry.

The artifacts in your portfolio should also provide readers/reviewers with a fair picture of how you understand ministry and how you would respond in a variety of pastoral and administrative contexts. If potential congregations or employers review your work, this is the information that they will want. Use the portfolio to help them understand who you are, what's important to you, what skills you have, and how you envision ministry in the world.

Commentary

In this professional context, a portfolio is more than a collection of artifacts. You also need to provide commentary and explanations. At the beginning of the portfolio, you should provide the reviewer with an introduction to the artifacts that they can find within the portfolio and a rationale for why you shared this particular set of items.

Like résumés, portfolios should be assembled in ways that highlight the skill sets that correspond with the skills needed for a particular position. For example, if you are seeking employment as a teacher, you'll want to highlight your educational background and curriculum-building skills. If you are seeking employment as a chaplain, you'll want to highlight your pastoral-care skills, your ability to handle emergencies, and your comfort with diversity.

Many e-portfolio programs allow you to customize which documents you want each potential reviewer to see. Take the time to think carefully about which documents apply to each context. Potential employers aren't impressed with the volume of material that you share with them. They are looking for quality.

While boards of ordained ministry and other employers are looking for skilled and thoughtful persons, they also know that people aren't perfect. Every portfolio and résumé will suggest weaknesses or areas of needed growth of a candidate. This is expected. What sets great portfolios and applications apart from mediocre or poor ones is the skill of the applicant in framing the information that the reviewer is receiving.

For example, it's possible that the evaluations of your sermons and your work in field education may indicate particular areas that you need to address going forward. Perhaps you need to strengthen your ability to speak in public, express your opinion without dominating a conversation, or explain complicated theological ideas. The question that will arise in the mind of the reviewer is, what did you do in response to this feedback? In addition to the artifacts, you'll need to anticipate these questions in the mind of the reviewer and address them in the commentary that you include with the portfolio. You may want to create a single document that provides some basic commentary about each item in your portfolio. Or you may decide to create a limited number of documents that correspond to particular artifacts. Your commentary needs to provide an explanation of what you learned from the feedback and experience, how you changed your approach in subsequent events, and how those changes have impacted others.

Items that you think reveal weaknesses and make you look less than perfect aren't necessarily problematic if you can show how you took responsibility for your actions, learned from the situation, and changed your behavior because of those experiences. Reviewers of your application materials will notice failed courses or a semester when all the courses are labeled "withdrawal." Boards of ordained ministry will read carefully evaluations from field-education supervisors and lay committees. As a result, you are better served if you address those items in your portfolio introductory commentary. If you are not using a portfolio, these items should be addressed in your cover letter.

In the same way, you should draw the reviewer's attention to the areas where you have excelled, successes that you have achieved, and awards that you have received. You should find ways to highlight comments in your preaching or field-education evaluations that identify your strengths and gifts for ministry. These kinds of comments are particularly helpful because they are direct assessments of your work and potential for future contributions in your place of work.

JOB APPLICATIONS, PROFILES, RÉSUMÉS, AND CURRICULA VITAE

The application process for positions can vary greatly. Some employers require a job application. Others require a résumé or curriculum vitae and cover letter. Larger denominations require applicants to use an online profile system. A potential employer needs to be able to trust you. All the information that you share in these documents and processes must be truthful and accurate, but each document comes with slightly different expectations. You need to know the differences among these documents.

Applications

Many applications for jobs, grants, and scholarships require all applicants to complete an application. When completing an application, you are expected to include every job and every school attended, unless otherwise stated. For example, if the application asks for your job history, you must list every position that you have held, regardless of how short the position lasted. In addition, you should be careful not to hide any details about an earlier position. For example, a person applying for a position at Planned Parenthood might decide not to list a one-year position after college with Students for Life of America. It's understandable for the applicant to be concerned about how the employment history will appear to the potential future employer, but hiding employment history will undermine an applicant's credibility. In this particular example, the applicant should address employment history directly in the cover letter.

If an employer realizes after hiring you that you have withheld, hidden, or lied about relevant information regarding your past, you will likely lose your position.

Profiles

Many denominations now require all those authorized for ministry to create an online profile inside the denominational profile database. For the profile, similar to a portfolio, the clergyperson or clergy candidate completes a list of required questions and submits important professional artifacts. Search committees and denominational leaders are then able to search the online system for ministers who would make a good match for a particular position. Churches with open positions are also expected to create profiles so that those looking for positions are able to see what is available.

Be sure to keep your profile updated. You never know who may be looking for someone with your gifts, skills, and background.

Résumés and Curricula Vitae

A résumé and a curriculum vitae (CV) are similar. Both are professional documents by which you present to potential employers your employment history, educational background, and achievements. They are unlike an application or profile in that you get to decide how the information is presented and what information you are going to share. This means that you don't have to include your job at the Dairy Queen when you were finishing your MDiv degree, unless you decide to do so.

In brief, a curriculum vitae is a comprehensive listing of your professional details. There are many books and websites you can consult for help in the preparation of your curriculum vitae. Every professional should have one and should update it on a regular basis, at least once a year. How you arrange the information in the CV will depend on how you understand your vocation and ministry. If you understand yourself as a pastor, you'll want your pastoral positions at the front of the document. If you are an educator, you'll want your academic degrees and your teaching experience at the front. Academic positions require the submission of a CV and cover letter as part of the application process.

Even if you don't think you'll ever need such a document, it's a helpful way to keep track of how you have spent your time professionally. For many of us, it's tedious to keep track of every time we have been a guest preacher or taught a workshop. Keeping an up-to-date CV helps you keep all this information in one place.

Résumés are not necessarily comprehensive in their coverage. Rather, the applicant carefully selects details from his or her professional background that directly address the desired skill sets and experience of a particular job announcement. Résumés are typically helpful when looking for a staff position in a church, company, or organization. The key is to make sure that you review your résumé in light of each application. The more the document is crafted to address the needs of a specific position, the more likely it is that your application will be moved to the next level of the process. If you are searching for an academic position, use a CV, not a résumé.

When you construct your résumé, make sure that what you highlight at the front of the document speaks to the requirements and expectations of the advertised position. If you are applying for a board-certified chaplain position, be sure to list your degrees and training at the beginning. Don't lead with your previous work experience, unless you already have experience working in a similar position.

There are many books and websites that can guide you in the creation of your résumé. You can also find examples of good and bad CVs and résumés online. Once you have completed a solid draft, share the document with trusted colleagues and a mentor or adviser. CVs and résumés should be free from any errors in grammar and formatting. When you need to supply a hard copy of these documents, be sure to print it on high-quality paper. If you need to submit them electronically, be sure to share versions that can't be distorted or changed when sharing by e-mail. If you send a document as Word document, it's likely that the document will be distorted when the potential employer opens it up. If possible, avoid submitting these documents by FAX; CVs and résumés that arrive by FAX rarely make a good appearance.

COVER LETTERS

Cover letters are often required at some point in a job application process. Even if you are using a denominational profile system, you'll likely need to write a letter to the potential community about your desire for the position and what makes you qualified and worthy of consideration.

At the beginning of an application process, the most important thing to remember is that the goal is to get to the next step of the employer's process. In other words, you want the cover letter and CV or résumé to gain you an interview. During the interview, they will get a clearer sense of why you are qualified, and you will get a better sense of whether you want to work in that community or organization. Even if you think you know a lot about the institution, getting more data about the expectations for the position is important. Your documents should convince the readers that they would benefit from hearing more about how you can support the work and mission of that institution.

There are countless resources available about how to create an appropriate cover letter, usually providing good and bad examples. Nevertheless, here are few tips to keep in mind:

—Address entry level and midlevel positions in a one-page cover letter.
—Use the letter to tell important parts of your story that would benefit them. Point out one or two aspects of your background or skills that would serve this employer well. Tell them what value you would offer to them.
—Don't write about how the job would be good for you. That may be true, but that's not their priority at this stage of the process.
—Address any noticeable issues in your CV or résumé, for example, lapses in employment, poor grades, poor evaluations, or lack of experience. Explain what you learned during your time without employment or what you learned from a failure or unsuccessful moment. Share how you now do things differently because of what you learned.
—Let them know that you would appreciate an opportunity to talk with them further about the position and how you can serve their needs.
—If it's important that your job search be treated confidentially in these initial stages, make that clear in the cover letter. If you are considering a new position, your current employer should hear this news directly from you and when the timing is right. That's usually at the final stages, when your application is being publicly considered by a congregation or institution during an on-site visit. You don't want your current employer to be caught off guard.

In the end, you want your application to stand out from the rest in the stack. When a selection committee is looking at fifty to a hundred applications for a single position, your application needs to be engaging, professional, succinct, and perfect. Your materials should look as perfect as you can make them, so as not to distract the reviewers. They won't concentrate on how gifted you are when your documents are poorly formatted and your name is misspelled. (Yes, I've seen this happen.)

REFERENCES

Every job-search process requires that you provide either a list of references with contact information or letters from your references. Furnish the potential employer with the information that they request. If they ask for names and contact information, do not send letters. Follow the directions in the job posting. If the announcement is unclear, inquire about what the organization would prefer.

As you consider who would make a good reference, think carefully about which people will have the most potential for influence with the organizations where you are applying. Every reference person may not be a wise choice for every position. You'll need about five or six people who are willing to be a reference for you. For each application you'll need to select the right combination of references that will appeal to each search committee.

Ideally a potential reference will tell you if they don't think they are the right person to help you. However, it's your responsibility to determine which reference will work best for each application. For example, one of your favorite professors could have been a new faculty member who is a recent doctoral graduate. That professor may be a good reference if you applying to the graduate school from which they recently graduated. If you are seeking a pastoral position, the new professor may not be well known enough to have a significant impact on your application.

Whenever you list a reference in your application materials, be sure to confirm in advance with your potential reference that they are willing to remain a reference. As you move into the job-search process, keep your references informed about the positions for which you are applying. If you haven't done this, your reference is likely to reveal to the person calling that they didn't know you were applying for the position. Even worse, if you list someone as a reference without asking them first, this fact will surface when the potential employer contacts the reference. This lack of care on your part will be interpreted negatively by the search committee.

You should supply all your references with your updated CV or résumé. If you ask them to write a letter of recommendation, send them the job description, your cover letter, and an addressed and stamped envelope. If you know that a potential employer is going to contact your references, send them all the same information. Give your references all the information they need to help you. In some cases you may need them to emphasize particular skill sets that you would bring to a position. Don't be afraid to let your references know how they can be helpful to you. You don't need to inform them at every step of your process. That would be too much. But you want them to have everything they need.

When you are offered a position, express your gratitude to your references for their support and assistance. If they agreed to be a reference for you, they will be invested in your success. Good references can have significant impact on a search process. Treat your references well.

INTERVIEWS

The interview stage can take many different forms. Fundamentally, the interview is a structured conversation meant to help you and the institution assess whether there is a good fit between you and the congregation or organization. If you are anxious about getting your first position or getting a new one, it is tempting to be completely focused on getting the job, regardless of whether it is a good fit or not. Resist that temptation. Instead, remember that a good fit is just as important to you as it is to the searching institution. If you have been asked to sit for an interview, their interest is piqued. Relax a bit and turn your attention to taking an honest, deep look at whether taking the position would allow you and them to flourish. If it won't, then you don't want to pursue the position any further.

In many cases the hiring body will want to do a preliminary set of interviews over the phone or with video conferencing. From this initial round the search committee will decide which candidates they want to bring on-site. In some cases the search committee will do the initial round of interviews on-site or off-site at a hotel. Wherever and however that initial interview takes place, treat it as a face-to-face interview.

The goal of this stage of the process is to see if you would be a good fit for the position, both from your perspective and from theirs. Below you'll find general guidance on the interview process. There are many resources on job seeking available, and you should consult them as well.

Preparation

Review all the documents that the search committee has shared with you. Read the job description carefully and note any places where you need more information or clarity. Bring a copy of the job description with you to the interview.

Ask your contact person at the institution about who will be participating in the conversation and how long the interview is supposed to last. Research each participant on the institution's website, and make notes for yourself about their position and how they would interact with the person in the position being posted.

Study the website of the institution, and search online for additional information. Look for the stated mission and vision statements and make a note of them. They can come in handy during the conversation.

If you are meeting face-to-face, be sure to have a copy of your CV or résumé or profile information with you. Bring several additional copies just in case someone in the interview needs it. Be sure to print those documents on résumé-quality paper. If you are meeting online or over the phone, be sure that your documents are available for viewing.

Prepare a list of three or four questions to ask the interviewers at the end of the conversation. You may have more questions on your mind, but some can wait until you get to the next stage. At this moment it's important to ask the questions that will help you assess whether you would feel comfortable in the position. It's standard practice to allow time for the applicant to ask questions at the end of the interview. If they ask you for your questions at the beginning, suggest that you wait until later in the conversation. You don't know what they are going to share in the interview, and you don't want to waste your questions.

When it comes time for you to ask your questions, go from the simplest to the most complex. This allows you to strengthen the relationship before heading into more difficult items. Here are a few examples of questions you could ask if they haven't been addressed earlier:

—How is the person in this position evaluated?

— What do you think are the most critical things the person in this position needs to do in the first ninety days?

— Who are the people that I would work with on a daily basis?

— What is your time line for the next steps of the hiring process?

Equally important to consider is what *not* to ask at this point. This is not the moment to ask about salary, benefits, or accommodations. They may be on your mind, but now is not the time to ask those questions. All those questions should be saved until it's time to negotiate an agreement. Organizations are more willing to make accommodations or changes to the compensation package, once they are interested in a particular candidate.

Sometimes a search committee or application process will ask you to share your salary requirements or expectations. In my experience, it's best to wait as long as possible before discussing salary. Tell them that your first priority is to understand the position and to get a sense of whether you would be a good fit. Salary isn't the only determining factor in the job-search process. As we will discuss later in this chapter, the right position includes quality of life, job location, benefits, and many other items. You and the search team could miss out on a great opportunity if you focus too quickly or solely on the salary amount.

A second temptation to avoid is presenting yourself as a problem. Those new to the job-search process can easily undermine their potential for a position because they think the employer would never hire a person with their particular qualities. People who have been minoritized are particularly vulnerable to this temptation. For example, if you are a same-gender-loving person, don't ask the search committee if you would be welcome in the organization. If this is a concern that you bring to this particular organization, mention something that would indicate your sexual orientation, and watch how people respond. If you have a spouse or partner, allow yourself to mention it as anyone might in casual conversation. You can then assess how people respond to that revelation without making your sexual orientation a problem for them.

Dress professionally, even if the interview is over the phone. Wear what you would be expected to wear in the position for which you are applying. That is to say, look the part. Wearing your interview clothing will help you remember the importance of the conversation. If you don't know what's appropriate for an interview of this type, consult with someone who holds a similar position.

If you are doing the interview from a distance, be sure to reduce all noise and distraction on your side. If you have children or pets, ask someone to take care of them during the interview. Take the interview in a quiet room. This is not a conversation you should have on your cell phone in a coffee shop.

During the Interview

You'll likely have several people participating, and you'll need to assess how long your answers should be. There is no simple equation for how long an answer should be, but your answers should be focused, concrete, and constructive. If you are concerned that your answers are too short, ask them if they would like to hear more details from you.

When you respond to questions, make eye contact with each person in the room. Even though one person has provided the question, the answer is for everybody. Each member of the interview team matters, and each one will have a voice in the hiring process. Don't ignore any of them.

At the end of interview, someone from the committee should tell you the next steps in the process. If they don't, ask them. If the interview experience has helped you to see that you would be a good fit for the position, let the interview team know that you look forward to hearing from them and would appreciate the opportunity to learn more about the organization and those involved.

If you are meeting face to face, make sure to shake hands and make eye contact with each person as you enter and leave the interview space.

Follow-Up to Interview

Express your gratitude to the church or organization for the opportunity to interview for the position. You can do that by a handwritten note, an e-mail, or a phone call. Many job guides will suggest the handwritten note. You can't go wrong with that. But ultimately, what's most important is that the gratitude is genuine and expressed well.

If they don't ask you back for the next interview or the on-site visit, you should still express your gratitude for being allowed to interview for the position. Do not complain or lament the fact that you didn't get the position. It's unprofessional and counterproductive. And sometimes the first choice candidate doesn't take the position or takes it but doesn't work out. When this happens, the search team may go back to the other people in the top tier of their process, which means they could call you back at a later time.

THE ON-SITE VISIT

Much of what applies to the first level of interviews also applies to the on-site visit. If you are candidating for a pastoral ministry position, the on-site visit is a critical part of the process. In some traditions the church will bring in only one candidate. In others, they will bring two or three different ministers to visit.

Here are a few additional pointers that apply to these visits:

— Remember that from the moment you arrive, the interview begins. You are on display the entire time. If you are housed with a family during the visit, assume that everything you say and do is part of the interview process, regardless of what they say. Whenever you are with people from the institution, your behavior and speech are being evaluated.

— Be prepared for a variety of different events as part of the visit. Ideally the church will send you an itinerary in advance so that you can prepare. Even if an event is more casual, that doesn't mean it's time for you to break out the shorts and flip-flops. Save that kind of casualness for another time.

— Pay attention to time. The congregation will likely assign you a host for the visit. Be prepared to follow the host's lead on when and where you are supposed to appear. Don't assume that you know what is acceptable for this specific context. If you seek and heed the guidance of the host, you'll be fine.

— If you are applying to be a pastor, you'll probably be expected to preach, among other speaking expectations. Prepare an original sermon for this particular community. You need to do your sermonic homework and to know something about the community. If you preach a sermon crafted for another community, the congregation will catch this. When they do, they are likely to assume that this interview wasn't a priority for you.

— If you are introverted, prepare yourself for an extended period of public engagement. You would do well to build in a few moments to spend by yourself, but you may not have many options.

Preaching at the worship service, greeting people afterward, participating in a public luncheon, and then a meeting with the search committee will all happen with little chance for a break. Find a few moments first thing in the morning to be alone, review your sermon and other notes, and pray.

— Express your gratitude to the congregation or organization and to the search committee.

NEGOTIATING TERMS OF CALL

Once a congregation or organization has determined that they want to invite you to take the position, they will contact you, most likely by phone. When they call, they may begin talking about the salary and benefits package. Listen carefully to what they are sharing, and then ask them to send you the offer in writing. Don't accept the offer immediately, no matter how happy you are to receive it. Express your gratitude for being invited to take the position, and ask them when they need to hear back from you with a decision. They will likely give you a few days to a week to make the decision. The larger the position, the more time they will offer. If taking the position requires a major move for you and your family, you'll need time to think through all the details. Use the time to consider whether you think you are a good fit for the position. Do you feel called to this position and to this community or organization? Do you have any concerns about taking the position that need to be addressed in advance? Once you have determined that the position is a good fit, you can begin thinking about the salary and benefits, often known as "terms of call."

When it comes to negotiating the terms of call, there are many possibilities to consider and different approaches among denominations. In some cases, there is no negotiation needed, because the denomination determines the exact terms of the appointment, including salary and benefits. If you belong to such a denomination, make sure you know the terms while you are in seminary. If you don't know how your denomination handles the terms of call, find out. Contact your mentor or your liaison with the denomination about how the terms are determined or negotiated.

If you don't already have a tax adviser and you are ordained or intend to be ordained, you should find one who knows how to file and handle taxes for clergy. Tax preparation for clergy is more complicated because there are additional benefits available for clergy. In addition, clergy can be hired as employees of a church or organization, or they can be considered self-employed. There are significant tax differences that you should explore with your tax adviser. If you need help finding someone, ask clergy friends if they have anyone to recommend. You can also ask your denominational representatives for suggestions.[2]

Some denominations do not determine the exact terms of call for each positon but publish guidelines for congregations and organizations. This information is public, and you should locate it. The fact that the denomination has published guidelines doesn't mean that every offer will follow them. Congregations that are struggling financially may not be able to offer what the guidelines suggest. This doesn't mean that you shouldn't take the position. You should know, however, what is considered acceptable compensation in your denomination. You may decide that the position is ideal for you and that there are other benefits in the terms of call that outweigh a lower salary. For example, if you know that the salary is significantly less than what the guidelines propose, you may want to raise the idea of making the position part-time instead of full-time. If you go that direction, be sure that the number of hours correlates with the salary offered.

A large number of clergy, clergy candidates, and those applying for positions in other sectors will be expected to negotiate the terms of their employment or call. Below is a list of things to consider when looking at the entire package. If you are looking at a position in a denominational church, you should also inquire with your denominational office for a list of items that could be part of the terms of call. If you are applying for another type of position or in a church that is nondenominational, this list will provide you the necessary items to consider.

Elements to Consider When Negotiating Terms of Call

Salary. How much is the salary? To what extent does it correlate with work required, including full-time or part-time employment? What is the payment schedule? If the congregation offers housing, this will affect the salary amount. Find out the going rate for housing in that location as you consider these two items.

Housing. Does the position come with housing? Some congregations have a parsonage or rectory for the pastor and the pastor's family. If the congregation has a house, they will likely expect you to live there. If you want to live in another location, they are not likely to raise your salary in light of your not living in their house.

Pension/Retirement. How much is paid toward retirement? Is there an option for the pension to be paid into an account that you are bringing from another position? Larger denominations will have their own pension plans that will follow you from position to position.

Health Care. How much health care is covered? Does it include dental and vision? Are you expected to pay a portion of the monthly payment? What are the copays?

Continuing Education. If the position is full-time, does it allow for days away from the office for continuing education? How many days? Most clergy are expected to do continuing education every year. Is there money budgeted for the costs of continuing education?

Denominational Conferences. Will the congregation pay for your attendance at denominational conferences? Usually they include a specific amount in the budget each year. You would be responsible for overages. Because some denominations require clergy to attend general conferences of the denomination, this is an important part of the agreement and should be spelled out in detail. Even if the position is part-time, you may be able to negotiate some support for conference attendance.

Office Space and Equipment. Does the position include office space? Will they provide a computer, printer, and other office equipment? Will they provide you with a cell phone? Is there an administrative assistant? What other office staff are there?

Vacation and Weekly Schedule Expectations. What are the expectations for your weekly schedule? Are you expected to hold regular office hours? How much paid vacation time are you allowed each year? Will vacation time increase with years of service? Part-time positions may include time off but not paid vacation.

Spiritual Retreats. Does the agreement include time and support, beyond time for vacation and continuing education, for an annual retreat? How much time and how much funding?

Sabbaticals. Does the position include a sabbatical? How often? Is it paid, unpaid, or partially paid?

Evaluations. Who will evaluate you in this position? How often will it occur and who will see it?

Separation. As odd as it feels to talk about it at the beginning, the agreement needs to outline how a separation or termination will be handled. How much notice does either party need to give? Would severance be included if the institution decided to release you from employment? If so, how is severance calculated? If the position is at a large institution, it will likely have a staff handbook that addresses all these items. The terms of call would simply refer to that document.

Relocation Expenses. To what extent will the institution cover your moving expenses, should that be necessary? If they do cover some or all moving expenses, do you need to submit a specific number of quotes from moving companies? Some organizations will offer reimbursement for moving expenses up to a definitive amount. Others will offer you a determined amount up front. In that case you could keep any remaining funds, if there are any. Keep in mind that few organizations will support relocation expenses for part-time positions.

REACHING AN AGREEMENT

Once you have received the offer in writing, you'll need to consider how all the pieces work together. In many cases the initial offer should be close to what you had expected, and only a few minor changes will be needed. If that's not the case, you'll need to prioritize what is most important to you. It wouldn't be wise to ask for an increase in salary, more vacation time, an increase in relocation expenses, and a new computer. Given your personal situation, more time off may be more valuable to you and your family than a larger salary. Or your relocation expenses may be larger than usual because you are moving from Florida to Alaska to take the position. Identify what's most important to you, and negotiate those few items. Remember that the organization is working with a finite amount of money to cover relocation and all compensation expenses. For smaller organizations there is often very little room for negotiating when it comes to salary or other cash expenses. Instead, they may be able to offer more flexible hours or more vacation time.

If you are in the position of negotiating an agreement for terms of call, you may want to consult an attorney. Attorneys can help you spot important information that is missing or potentially problematic in the agreement. It's easy to overlook the details when you are excited about the prospects of having a position. If the position is significant, with a sizable compensation package, you'll certainly want to make sure that each item is clearly addressed. You'll be grateful in the long run.

I have a word of caution about utilizing an attorney in the process.

Use the attorney as your consultant. Remember that you are the person who is making the commitment—not the attorney. Furthermore, don't talk about consulting an attorney when you are negotiating the terms with the organization. Mentioning this can give the organization the impression that you would become litigious if things didn't go well. This isn't a good way to begin a new relationship. Using the attorney is simply to help you make informed decisions.

LEARNING AND DEVELOPING AS A WAY OF LIFE

Continuing education may be the last thing on your mind as you finish your degree. Nonetheless, every professional is expected to keep learning about their field. We all expect our medical doctors to keep abreast of new medicines and treatments. We should expect the same of our spiritual leaders.

As you finish your degree and enter your first position, you'll begin to identify areas where you need ongoing education or additional education. Consider the situation for those who will preach on a regular basis. They will need ongoing education and biblical interpretation resources. Ask your Bible professors about the best ways to stay abreast of developments in the field. Ask them the extent to which you should invest in your own commentaries. One of the best pieces of advice I got on this point was to buy two or three commentaries on each of the Gospels. That investment was particularly helpful because my first clergy assignment was far away from a theological library.

Ask your professors in each area for suggestions about how to keep updated in their field. Which conferences are worth attending on a regular basis? Are there schools or organizations that offer worthwhile continuing education in that field?

Every graduate will discover gaps in their education once they begin working. No degree program covers everything a person needs to know. Moreover, some skills or ideas are best learned on the job, at the moment when you need them. For example, learning how to create a strategic plan is necessary, but you may not encounter this task right away in your work. When the time comes to face this task, you'll appreciate some in-time learning as you move through the process.

There shouldn't be a time when you aren't learning and developing as a spiritual leader. Some of what you need to learn will be generated externally by the tasks assigned to you. Others, however, will emerge from within yourself. You'll discover a need to learn how to pray in new ways. The former ways may have worked well for you, but the demands of ministry and the charge to pray for others will affect you. There are numerous resources that you can consult, or you can seek out spiritual conferences that provide guidance, space, and insight for nourishing your spiritual development.

You will likely be challenged to deal with your own loneliness, discouragement, and disappointment. Working with a spiritual director and making an annual retreat are helpful ways of dealing with these common challenges for spiritual leaders. Don't wait until you are in crisis to find a spiritual director or to make a retreat. Make both a part of your spiritual practice.

Another way to deal with the loneliness and isolation that often come with ministerial leadership is to join a support group for pastors or a local ministerium. A ministerium is an ecumenical group of pastors in a local area who gather for support, information sharing, sermon preparation, or sometimes shared programming. Each one is different, and each one has its own vibe. Those who are more extroverted will often find these gatherings helpful. Others find them draining. Check out the local ministerium and see if it works for you. If it doesn't, seek out a clergy support group. If you can't find one in your area, look online or check with your seminary. It's possible that they sponsor a group in your area. If all this fails, make the effort to visit your seminary classmates and spend quality time together talking about your experiences of ministry. You need support, and they need support.

Completing your theological degree is not the end of your theological education. In fact, it is not the longest part of your education. Living and working as a spiritual leader will draw you deeper and deeper into the challenges and the beauties of seeing the world with a theological framework. Enjoy the process and all the invitations and graces that God offers to you at each step of the way.

Appendix 1
Applying to Theological Schools

Once you have decided to apply to degree programs at theological schools, it's time to prepare the application packets. This appendix offers some tips regarding the various components of an application.

As stated in earlier chapters, you should talk with your home pastor and the appropriate denominational officer if you are interested in leadership within that community. If you haven't done so already, look at the exercises outlined in chapter 3 to become aware of what is expected of you by your denomination. Depending on the guidelines of the denomination, enrolling in a seminary before seeking out the guidance and approval of the leadership of the church can preclude official endorsement and support by the denomination. Be aware that some endorsement processes can take up to a year to complete. You need to factor that time into your planning.

As we begin this discussion, the assumption is that through the discernment process you have identified two or three schools offering the theological degree appropriate to the form of ministry that you are pursuing and that you are ready to apply to those schools. You may have your heart set on one particular school, but it's much wiser to apply to at least two or three schools. Because each school has a different ethos and application process, each application will provide you with opportunities to clarify your own educational priorities. And you may not get accepted at the school of your choice and may need a plan B.

TIPS ON APPLICATION COMPONENTS

Screenings or Required Testing

Some schools require all applicants to undergo certain kinds of screenings or testing, at the applicant's expense. For example, some schools require a psychological and/or vocational assessment of all applicants. Sometimes those assessments are done as part of the application process but are not used in the decision-making process of the school. Instead, the results of the assessment are used to help the student in the formation program. In other cases, a school may require mental-health screenings of all applicants. Again, the screenings may be performed as part of the application process but be used to help the admitted student, not as part of the admissions decision.

In other cases, a school may require standardized tests to assess the academic readiness of an applicant. The most common test is the Graduate Record Examination (GRE). It is most commonly used by theological schools embedded in a university that has school-wide standards that must be followed. Other schools will require educational testing only of applicants who do not have a bachelor's degree. In these cases, the testing will help the admissions committee of a school assess the extent to which an applicant is prepared for graduate studies.

In the case of psychological, vocational, or educational assessments, you always have the choice not to release the results to a school. In order for the results to be released, you must agree to release the results. Because this information is personal and could be reviewed by several people within an institution, it's important for you to know who will review this information and how it will be used in the process. Concerning the educational testing, it is important for you to ask if there is a threshold score required for accepting students into a program.

I would strongly suggest that you review the results of any testing or screening *before* releasing the results to a school or another party for review. Because this adds time and expense to the process, it's important to identify as quickly as possible whether a school requires any type of screening or testing as part of the application process. Don't allow yourself to be pressured into releasing the results until you have had a chance to review them.

Essay/Writing Sample

The application essay, sometimes called a writing sample, is what most admissions committee members read first and scrutinize the most. Follow carefully the instructions for the essay. If the request is for three pages, don't submit a five-page essay. Applicants who don't follow the instructions raise concerns for the committee members.

What are admissions committee members looking for in the application essay? That's a difficult question to answer. Each school will have a set of institutional values that will shape the lens of the readers. For example, if a school is committed to a particular theological concern or concerns, a committee may be looking to see how well you will embrace that set of values. Having said that, there are some things for which most committees will be listening.

— *Self-Knowledge.* To what extent does the applicant know herself or himself? Can they identify their social location?

— *Teachability.* To what extent does an applicant demonstrate openness to learning and being challenged?

— *Contextual Awareness.* To what extent is the applicant aware of the challenges and opportunities within the church, denominations, and the world?

— *Ability to Be a Team Player.* To what extent will this applicant work well with student colleagues?

— *Leadership.* To what extent does the applicant demonstrate an ability to lead others?

— *Sensitivity to Diversity.* To what extent is this applicant aware of the various forms of diversity—for example, theological, racial, denominational, gender, sexual orientation, and ethnic—and willing to engage that diversity in the educational process?

Admissions committees aren't looking for perfection. They are looking for the extent to which an applicant is aware of herself or himself and the larger dynamics at work in the church and world. Furthermore, the schools will have their own measures for the amount and quality of awareness that they require for acceptance.

Because the application essay is often considered a writing sample, you must be the actual author of the essay. The essay should demonstrate the highest quality of writing that you can offer. While it is wise and appropriate to get feedback from trusted colleagues, you should not ask anyone else to write or to revise an application essay. Your voice should be clear and distinct in the text. That is to say, the essay should sound like you and make sense when read in light of your larger life story.

References

Most applications will require three or four reference letters, which should be sent directly to the school or in sealed envelopes along with the application. Most schools will have guidelines for the references. For example, most programs will ask for a letter from your pastor or denomination.

When you ask someone to be a reference, you are asking a favor. Before you ask, consider how long and how well the person has known you. What do you think she or he will say? Does he or she have reservations about your decision to apply to a theological school? If the reference hasn't known you for a long time or is likely to have reservations about your application, you may want to ask someone else. If you know that he or she is going to include a particularly critical remark and you still want her or him to write a letter for you, you should address that issue in your cover letter. See my discussion of the cover letter later in this chapter for more details.

Be sure to provide the referring person with all the pertinent school guidelines and deadlines. Share with her or him a copy of your application essay, even if it's just a draft. This will help the writer to understand what you are hoping to accomplish by pursuing the degree. If the person writing the letter needs to mail the letter directly to the school, address the envelope and attach the necessary postage. Make it as easy as possible for him or her to help you.

Transcript(s)

All applications will require transcripts from your bachelor's degree program, which will also validate the conferral of your bachelor's degree. If you have attended more than one college, you'll need to request a transcript from each school that you attended. If you already have a graduate degree or some credits achieved at the graduate level, you'll be asked to send official transcripts for these as well.

If you have an associate's degree or not enough undergraduate credits to complete a bachelor's degree, you'll need to supply a transcript with this coursework too. If you haven't completed your undergraduate degree but have a significant amount of professional work experience, a school may be willing to classify you as having a bachelor's equivalent. This isn't a degree or a classification that you can take to another school, but it may affect your chance at a successful application and your funding options.

If you are not able to supply a requested transcript, you'll need to explain the issue in detail in your cover letter. In some cases, you'll need to resolve that issue before you'll be able to successfully apply to a graduate program. See discussion of the cover letter later in this chapter.

Background Check

All schools will require a background check on applicants. The extent and method used will vary according to schools. The school will likely make the arrangements and expect you to reimburse them for the fee. Because students at theological schools are often in residence, even for a limited time, and may be required to do fieldwork that involves youth, they are required to take precautions.

Application Form

Like job applications, degree application forms require you to complete all the questions truthfully. Providing false or incomplete information on an application form can result in the decline of your application or a standards violation later in your academic career, if the deception is discovered.

If you think that some of your responses to the application questions may raise flags for the admissions officer or the committee, be sure to address those in the cover letter. See treatment of the cover letter later in this chapter.

Application Fee

Most schools will charge an application fee and a fee for a background check. Payment by check is typically expected. In some cases schools will offer discounts for early applications. If you aren't able to afford the application fee, take a second look at your finances and your plans to fund your graduate studies. An inability to pay the application fee will raise a red flag about your financial stability with the admissions staff at the seminary. If you need assistance coming up with the application fee, you'll need to make sure that you have a strong and clear financial plan to get you through the program and beyond.

Free Application for Federal Student Aid (FAFSA)

In order to apply for federal student aid, that is, student loans, or for scholarship funds, you'll need to complete this free application. The school will use the results of this application to determine if you qualify for need-based scholarship. The student-loan officer will also use this information to determine how much student-loan funding you are eligible for. Federal law requires all schools that participate in the federal student-aid program to provide loan counseling and education at the beginning and ending of your degree program.

If you have a student loan that is in default, you will not be eligible for additional student loans, and a school will likely not grant you scholarship funds until the loan is completely, officially out of default. Be aware that it can take six months or more to bring a loan out of default. Note that it is not the responsibility of the student loan office of the school to resolve your loan default. While they may be able to provide you with important information, it is your responsibility to address the loan issue.

See appendix 2 for more information and ideas about how to fund your education.

Cover Letter

Generally, applications to theological schools do not require a formal cover letter. Schools will make it clear if they do want one, but usually the other documents that they request cover the information that they are seeking. However, you may need to include a cover letter if there is anything in your packet that you know will be of concern to the committee. The readers will notice these details. If any of the following apply to your application, I suggest that you address them head-on in a cover letter:

— Failing grades
— Standards violations noted on transcripts
— Arrests
— Imprisonment
— Restraining order
— Bankruptcy
— Student loan default
— Student-loan indebtedness of $50,000 or more
— Issues shared by references
— Employment difficulties

It's impossible to predict how an admissions committee will interpret any of these matters or similar ones. They won't share with you what they think, either. All you will know is their final decision. In my experience, what a committee is looking for is how you have learned from an experience, and how you have changed your life because of what you learned. If an application includes important matters like these and you completely ignore those realities, a committee is not likely to admit you. If you include life difficulties and even failures but can demonstrate how you have used that experience to transform your life for the better, that's a powerful testimony and is likely to get the attention of the admissions committee.

Appendix 2
Funding Your Theological Education

LIVING AS A STUDENT AGAIN

Entering into a graduate theology program is a significant vocational decision. It's also a serious financial commitment.[1] If you feel strongly about applying to a theology degree program, it can be tempting to ignore the financial realities of the decision. I've heard some students spiritualize the decision, saying that God will make sure that everything works out. If God has indeed invited you to take the next step in your discipleship by attending seminary, God will support you in this endeavor. However, that doesn't mean that you don't have responsibilities too. Pursuing a life of ministry does not release you from paying attention to your finances or allow you to neglect your commitments.

It's also important to note from the start that if you are experiencing financial difficulties, entering a degree program will not solve them. Going back to school could make your financial situation more complex.

Entering a degree program will require many lifestyle changes. How you spend your resources is one place that may require some adjustments. Theology students should not live in poverty, but they will likely need to live more simply. Specialty coffees, gym memberships, cell-phone plans, cable plans, eating out, and visits to the salon are a few examples of expenses that may need to be curtailed or limited while in school. Family vacations and other large expenses may need to be postponed or simplified while you are in school. Whether you are single or have a family, you'll need to find less expensive ways to meet your needs and to have fun while you are a student.

In chapter 3 we discussed the option of on-campus housing. Living on campus can have significant financial benefits. If you are currently renting an apartment, you should definitely consider moving to campus. Find out what the school charges for housing and what is included. You are likely to save on rent, utilities, and commuting expenses.

The realities of student debt and the challenges of funding seminarians are being discussed throughout the church in the United States. Congregations and denominations are examining their responsibilities for supporting the education of their future clergy and seeking to develop better structures to facilitate that support. This is good news for seminarians. Church leaders are becoming more aware of the financial challenges of seminarians and want to help students manage the financial burdens of a theological education. Seminarians should not hesitate to reach out to their denominational leaders for support, including financial support. This being said, you need to be deliberate about how you manage the financial requirements of a theological degree program. You cannot shift your financial responsibilities onto your seminary, denomination, or congregation.

CREATING A SPENDING PLAN

The first step in successfully funding your theological education is to create a yearly spending plan. Ideally you would create such a plan before you commit to a particular school and program so that you are confident that you can afford to attend seminary. Each school can provide you with a list of general costs associated with its program, which include tuition, fees, housing, food, and books. Because the cost of living and other expenses can vary greatly according to the location of the school and the nature of the program, online or residential, you will need to obtain the list of expenses from each school. Depending on your situation, you'll need to add into your calculations other costs like commuting expenses, computer needs, and tutoring fees.

Once you have your complete list of expenses, you can calculate how much money you need to fund your degree and when you need the money to be available. You will be required to pay some expenses up front. Others will be spread across the semester or year. For example, many seminaries bill residential students for housing by the semester. Tuition and fees must also be paid at the beginning of the semester. This means you'll have a large bill to pay at the beginning of each semester. Books are another significant expense, but they can be purchased when you need them or borrowed from a library.

Most schools will not permit you to carry unpaid balances from one semester into another. In fact, federal law prevents you from using student loans designated for the current academic year to be used for expenses from previous years. You'll also be expected to keep your account current, if you want to get credit for your courses and be able to register for the following semester. Creating an accurate and realistic spending plan is an important step in keeping your finances stable while you are in school. If you don't know how much money you will need to spend, you won't be able to assess if you have enough to cover your costs. See the end of this appendix for additional resources to help you create your spending plan.

FUNDING RESOURCES

The goal is to complete your theological degree with as little debt as possible. Simply ensuring that you have enough money to cover all your expenses is not a satisfactory plan, because you could incur more student-loan debt than you will be capable of paying back in the future. Consequently, your strategy should begin by obtaining as much scholarship and grant money as possible before looking to other sources.

Here is a list of potential sources for funding your degree program.

Denominational Scholarships. If you are officially in care or your enrollment in seminary is officially sponsored by your denomination, you may be eligible for scholarship funds from your denomination. Some funds are dispersed on the regional level. Others are handled on the national or denominational level. You can ask your local pastor about these funds, but you'll likely need to contact the office that handles clergy education for the denomination. Be sure to ask about available funds at both the regional and national levels. In some cases, you can get funding from both.

Local Church Scholarship. Your home congregation may have an education fund designed to assist students pursuing theological studies. Some churches have restricted endowments that were created many years ago for this purpose and remain unused. Often restrictions apply, so it's good to inquire about potential funds before you get too far into the application and admissions process. Some scholarships are limited to particular schools or require the person to be an officially sponsored candidate for ministry. Even if your church can't provide you with a scholarship, ask if there are ways in which the church or church members could help with smaller expenses, like textbooks or gasoline. Every bit of assistance you can gather means less money that you have to borrow.

Seminary Scholarships. Nearly all seminaries award scholarships. Some are based on merit, others on need. As part of your discernment process, ask about what scholarships are available. Some schools will have additional scholarship offerings based on denomination, gender, nationality, or sexual orientation. Schools won't indicate how much they would be able to offer you until you submit a complete application, including the Free Application for Federal Student Aid, better known as the FAFSA.

Federal Student Aid. The federal government offers aid to students in professional and graduate-degree programs through unsubsidized loans. In order for a student to obtain such a loan, the school must be approved for distributing such funds through Title IV of the Higher Education Act of 1965. If you intend to rely on federal student aid to help fund your education, make sure your school is approved. You can find all the information you need regarding student loans on the official website, www.studentloans.gov. The site includes calculators that allow a student to see projected loan-payment amounts.

Financial-aid offices of the school will be reviewing your financial need and your student-loan history. If you have a student loan in default, you will not be eligible for additional federal aid until the loan is out of default. The seminary will also require you to get the loan out of default before it will make any scholarship offers. In some cases, you won't be able to matriculate until the student loan is out of default, which could take six months or more.

Relying on federal aid to fund your program can be seductive. As long as you are making satisfactory progress and enrolling for at least the minimum number of qualifying credits, you can take advantage of federal loans However, the more money you borrow during your education, the greater your monthly payment will be after graduation. Depending on your entire financial situation, you could end up with a monthly loan payment that you won't be able to afford.

Here is an illustration about how the final cost of a degree can be increased exponentially by extending your time in the program and taking the largest loan amount possible.

Years in Program	Maximum Annual Loan Amount	Loan Subtotal*
Year 1	$20,500	$20,500
Year 2	$20,500	$41,000
Year 3	$20,500	$61,500
Year 4	$20,500	$82,000
Year 5	$20,500	$102,500
Year 6	$20,500	$123,000

*Figures for each student will vary greatly because these subtotals do not include scholarship funding or the interest incurred from your loan amounts.

Keep in mind that a student can take out up to $20,500 per year in federal loans as long as the student is taking a minimum of six credits. With this in mind, the student who goes full-time and completes an MDiv degree in three years will take out significantly less in student loans than the student who takes six years and takes out loans for six years. The table above stops at six years, but a student may need longer, depending on the number of credits required for graduation.

Student-loan debt is not discharged in bankruptcy. It essentially remains forever on your credit report if it is not paid.

Part-Time Job. Students who are attending school full-time and don't have a job may want to consider getting a part-time job. This isn't possible for everyone, given the other factors in a person's life. However, most schools have a limited number of student-worker positions available. Other options include seasonal positions over the holidays or during summer. Even if your financial situation dictates that you work while you are in school, you will need to assess how much time you can realistically allocate for school, work, and home life.

Credit Cards. Credit cards are not a wise way to finance your education. You may need to use them to purchase your textbooks, but they shouldn't be used to finance tuition and fees. If you do, you'll pay exorbitant interest rates. If you need to borrow money, investigate federal student aid. Before entering seminary, it would be wise to reduce any credit-card debt as much as possible.

Retirement Savings. Some students are pursuing a second or third career when they enter seminary and have retirement funds that they could use to help support their education. Because each person's situation is different, it's impossible to make a blanket recommendation. Before making the decision to deplete your retirement investments, consult with a trusted financial adviser. Depending on your age and the amount of money you have available, it could be wiser to pursue other options.

FINANCIAL AID OFFICE

Every school has at least one office that is charged with assisting students with their educational finances. The student loan counselor is a valuable resource and can give you feedback on your spending plan and your funding plan. In addition, many schools have a staff member who organizes educational events and mentoring regarding spending plans, credit, and financial literacy. Take advantage of these resources. If you can graduate with little or no additional educational debt, it will be worth the effort.

ADDITIONAL READING

Gobel, Reyna. *Cliff Notes Graduation Debt: How to Manage Student Loans and Live Your Life,* 2nd ed. New York: Houghton Mifflin Harcourt, 2014.

Openshaw, Jennifer. *Quick and Easy Budget Kit and Workbook.* Greenwich, CT: Family Financial Network, 2005.

Twist, Lynne. *The Soul of Money: Reclaiming the Wealth of Our Inner Resources.* New York: W. W. Norton, 2003.

Tyson, Eric. *Personal Finance for Dummies.* Hoboken, NJ: Wiley, 2012.

Notes

Chapter 1: Searching for a Meaningful Life

1. Patricia O'Connell Killen and John de Beer, *The Art of Theological Reflection* (New York: Crossroad, 1994), viii.

2. For an overview of various models of theological reflection, see John Trokan, "Models of Theological Reflection: Theory and Praxis," *Catholic Education: A Journal of Inquiry and Practice* 1, no. 2 (December 1997): 144–58.

3. This movement of experience, feelings, images, insight, and action is the way Killen and de Beer describe one pattern for theological reflection in *The Art of Theological Reflection*.

4. Thomas Merton, *My Argument with the Gestapo: A Macaronic Journal* (New York: Doubleday, 1969), 160–61, emphasis added.

5. Churches regularly call together discernment committees to help the community make a significant decision, e.g., calling a new minister, building a new sanctuary, or initiating a new outreach program. Trouble emerges quickly when the charge to the committee is unclear. Discernment committees pull together information and study the complete situation. They are typically asked to make recommendations, based on their work, to the leadership or the entire community, which is authorized to make the decision. If this isn't spelled out, discernment committees can drift into making decisions that they are not authorized to make.

Chapter 2: Envisioning Your Educational and Vocational Path

1. Charles R. Foster, et al., *Educating Clergy: Teaching Practices and Pastoral Imagination*, Carnegie Foundation for the Advancement of Teaching (San Francisco: Jossey-Bass, 2006).

2. See the Association of Theological Schools' website: 2013–2014 Annual Data Tables, http://www.ats.edu/uploads/resources/institutional-data/annual-data-tables/2013-2014-annual-data-tables.pdf.

3. In some traditions, seminarians are required to do a yearlong internship, which is basically a year of full-time supervised ministry. During the internship, the student may or may not be taking classes.

4. The Association of Theological Schools, www.ats.edu, emphasizes the importance of a community of learners throughout the degree standards. See the Association of Theological Schools, The Commission on Accrediting, *Degree Program Standards*, 2012.

Chapter 3: Discerning and Deciding

1. If you are thinking about ordination or authorized ministry in a denomination that is not currently your own, you may want to consider attending a church in that denomination before taking any additional steps. Most denominations will have a membership requirement to be fulfilled before it will consider officially supporting someone in a seminary program. If you are serious about pursuing ministry in that new denomination, it's wisest to consult with the denomination before applying to a seminary.

2. The Episcopal Church is also identified as a mainline Protestant church, but its process for authorizing clergy operates with some similarity to the Roman Catholic process.

3. Spiritual guidance is also known as spiritual companionship or spiritual direction.

4. Some denominations do authorize ministers for a single congregation or region. These ministers receive a license but are not ordained. Their ministry is typically limited to a specific local church or region. In some cases the denomination will restrict which religious rituals the licensed minister can perform.

5. Roman Catholic seminaries usually offer degrees and programs that are designed for the laity. Some of these schools also operate degree programs that are ecumenical. These programs, however, are separate from the degrees offered to prepare men to be priests.

6. See appendix 2, "Funding Your Theological Education," for more information.

7. See Paolo Freire's *Pedagogy of the Oppressed, 30th Anniversary Edition*, with an introduction by Ronaldo Macedo, trans. Myra Bergman Ramos (New York: Bloomsbury, 2000) for his critique of educational systems and their power to oppress people.

8. Elizabeth Liebert, *The Way of Discernment: Spiritual Practices for Decision Making* (Louisville, KY: Westminster John Knox Press, 2008). See chapter 2 of Liebert for all five foundations and their role in the discernment process and her outline of discernment practices.

9. Ibid., 23.

10. Ibid., 33.

Chapter 4: Learning What You Need to Know for Ministry

1. John Wesley, one of the leaders of the Methodist movement, identified human experience (collective, not individual) as one source for theological reflection.

2. Robert Orsi, *Between Heaven and Earth: The Religious Worlds People Make and the Scholars Who Study Them* (Princeton, NJ: Princeton University Press, 2005), 7–8.

3. I once knew a student who was missing morning classes on a regular basis because he couldn't get up in the morning. It wasn't a medical issue; he would stay up late and play video games. The student asked his faculty adviser if she would call and wake him up in the morning because he was having a hard time getting out of bed. She replied, "I'm not your mother."

Chapter 5: Cultivating the Practices of Ministry

1. Kathleen Cahalan, *Introducing the Practice of Ministry* (Collegeville, MN: Liturgical Press, 2010). Cahalan argues that even though all disciples receive charisms that they are called to use in service for the sake of God's reign, the word "ministry" should be reserved for those called to lead Christian communities. Those called to ministry are given specific charisms or gifts that empower them to serve God and God's people in this particular way.

2. In most Christian traditions, baptism is considered a significant moment in the life of a disciple. For some, it signifies that someone has entered the path of discipleship at an earlier moment. For others, baptism is one's entrance into discipleship. Either way, God gives each member of the body of Christ gifts for the good of the body and the sake of the reign of God.

3. Cahalan, *Introducing the Practice*, 5.

4. Ibid., ix.

5. "Sermon" is the more common word used in Protestant congregations to describe the moment when the minister addresses the community. "Homily" is typically used in Roman Catholic churches. While some practical theologians would argue that the terms represent different types of preaching, I would propose that the distinctions don't play themselves out so clearly in congregational life. We'll concentrate here on what elements they have in common.

6. See Eph. 6:12.

7. Edwin H. Friedman argues that the single determining factor of good leadership is the ability of a person to differentiate between what is good for the institution and what is good for the leader. There are no techniques or tricks that will make up for a leader's inability to differentiate. See Friedman, *A Failure of Nerve: Leadership in the Age of the Quick Fix* (New York: Church Publishing, 2007).

8. Examples of these courses are Presbyterian Polity, United Methodist Church Polity, Universal Fellowship of Metropolitan Community Churches Polity, and Baptist Polity.

9. One exception to this admonition is for the person who comes with significant administrative experience, particularly with churches or other similar nonprofits. People with other types of leadership experience or financial administration may qualify for an exception as well, but it will likely hinge on whether

a seminarian has experience with the ethical, theological, and leadership dimensions of institutional administration.

Chapter 6: Shaping an Identity for Ministry

1. In your theology classes, you will study and debate different theories of selfhood and identity. At the center of the debate is the extent to which our identities are given or created. You'll need to figure out for yourself where you are in that conversation. Some schools will profess very specific understandings of human identity that students will be expected to embrace if they wish to make satisfactory progress in the program.

2. James Thayer, "Krisis," in *Thayer's Greek-English Lexicon of the New Testament: Coded with Strong's Concordance Numbers*, Bible Hub, http://biblehub.com/greek/2920.htm.

3. Julia Cameron, *The Artist's Way* (New York: Putnam, 2002).

4. Natalie Goldberg, *Writing Down the Bones: Freeing the Writer Within*, 2nd ed. (Boston: Shambala, 2005).

5. Trent Gilliss, "Nadia Bolz-Weber Talks Tattoos, Resurrection, and God's Disruption," *On Being with Krista Tippett*, September 8, 2013, http://www.onbeing.org/blog/nadia-bolz-weber-talks-tattoos-resurrection-and-gods-disruption-video/5921.

6. Exod. 20:8.

7. Wayne Muller, *Sabbath: Restoring the Sacred Rhythm of Rest* (New York: Bantam, 1999), 2.

8. During my theological studies, I became very concerned about the lack of conversation regarding sexuality, spirituality, and ministry. Intuitively I knew that the integrity of my formation as a minister required that I do something about this need. I decided to invite another seminarian to join me in a series of planned conversations around these topics and their interconnection. We scheduled the first dialogue to take place during our class retreat. I didn't have any idea what this commitment would entail or how the conversation would go. We barely got started when I realized that I would need to share a lot more about myself than I had expected, if this conversation was going to become meaningful. I took the risk, and it made all the difference. My dialogue partner did the same. Those conversations, which took place over the course of one year, became the foundation of a friendship that has lasted for over twenty-five years. Our friendship became a core part of my theological development. When we talk now each month, we can dive directly into conversations about things that matter.

Chapter 7: Learning While Pastoring

1. In this situation, examples of people with a conflict of interest would be a relative or a spiritual guide.

2. See chapter 2 for more about CPE.

3. If you are considering whether to share some of the information that you are learning in class, you should digest the information yourself first. In that process, here are a few questions to consider: What's important to me about this idea or perspective? What question or questions does this idea or perspective generate for me? Why do I want to share this information with others? What do I hope will happen in the conversation? How do I think others will respond to this information? Am I prepared for the ways that people may respond?

Chapter 8: The Job-Search Process

1. These are a few of the questions we have used in the formation program at Lancaster Theological Seminary.

2. If these options fail, ask the bookkeeper for the denomination for a suggestion. That person will have connections with people in the field who know how to do taxes for clergy.

Appendix 2: Funding Your Theological Education

1. I suggest that before you make your final decision you talk with your accountant about your plans and your current financial situation.

Index

CPSIA information can be obtained
at www.ICGtesting.com
Printed in the USA
LVOW13s1944130318
569701LV00023B/265/P

9 780664 259501